MORO SHEEBA

MORO SHEEBA

By

BEATRICE TANNEHILL KING

Missionary to the Congo under the Africa Inland Mission

MOODY PRESS

CHICAGO

Printed in the United States of America

To

MY AFRICAN SISTERS IN CHRIST

who have dedicated their lives to the task

of making the Lord Jesus known

to their families and fellow women still in darkness

this book is

lovingly dedicated

PREFACE

THINGS NOT WRITTEN DOWN get lost and twisted in one," remarked a relative of Moro Sheeba's one day during the three weeks that I lived with her people at Awasi, questioning close relatives and friends that this story of her life might be accurate and complete.

Picture all of us crowded into the little mud hut where we worked—the evangelist, the subchief, the women of *Monkwenda,* the relatives. Mugasa and a village brother are sitting on chairs in front of me. Mugasa insists that every incident be put down in detail, and printed just so in the book. It is difficult to breathe, for both doors and the tiny window are jammed with boys and girls as fascinated by the stories as we are.

At times we dealt with matters so sacred that it seemed irreverent to be using the typewriter. As they remembered the heavenly fragrance of the life that had been lived in their midst, many were moved to renewed consecration to their Lord, so that the time would not have been lost even if the book had not been written. Some of the women whose hearts had been blessed, instead of the usual handshake, took my hand and gently bit my little finger in tender farewell as I left Awasi to return to my station.

Although my personal association with Moro Sheeba was close and much of what is recounted in the succeeding pages she told me herself during the years when we tramped the narrow African paths together in our mission of bringing the Gospel to our fellow women, I have deliberately sought to keep missionary activity out of the book as far as possible—for this is not the story of a missionary or even of a missionary work in Alurland. It is a testimony to the power of God to stamp His image upon a life that He has delivered from the darkness of heathenism.

Words and names of an unfamiliar tongue are inevitable in an account such as this, but they should offer no problem if they are sounded phonetically and the following pronunciation given to the vowels: a as in äh—e as long ā in āle—i as long ē in ēve—o as in ȯbey—u as o͞o in so͞on. We have spelled the heroine's name "Sheeba" to insure proper pronunciation; originally it was "Sheba."

I am deeply indebted to Miss Evelyn Woodsworth, who has edited the manuscript for me. Her prayerful aid and inspiration have greatly helped in getting this story ready for publication. My sincere appreciation goes also to those who took time to read the original draft of the book, and I gratefully acknowledge the value of their constructive criticism.

If the perusal of these pages creates in the heart of the reader a holy determination to live a more consistent, unselfish life for our Lord and a burning desire to do his or her part, by prayer or going, in getting the Gospel to Moro Sheeba's unreached fellow countrymen, then the purpose of recording her life story will have been accomplished.

BEATRICE TANNEHILL KING

Lindsay, California

CONTENTS

Chapter 1

THE PRICE OF A CHILD

THE NAME OF MORO SHEEBA is enshrined in loving memory in the hearts of many simple black folk who live on the hills of Alurland in the northeastern corner of the Belgian Congo. Eagerly they have made their contributions to the story related here, for the influence of this humble woman upon them is as fresh as it was in the days when she walked their paths with the Book of God in her hand. The power of her life can be accounted for only by the miraculous touch of the divine hand, the miracle best measured in contrast to the inheritance which was hers by nature.

Moro Sheeba's story begins in the village Pa Dolo at the time of the great famine when Moro's mother, Akelo, was a little girl. From the village Pa Dolo one could look across the rolling hills to Uganda, whence the Alurs had migrated many years before. If one followed the foot trails that led from it in an easterly direction, a few hours' walk would bring one to the northern shore of Lake Albert. The sands and escarpments, the forests, plains, and hills that surrounded the great inland lake had been familiar to generations of dusky dwellers who looked upon them as their own. But in the latter part of the nineteenth century, explorers from the white man's world began to penetrate this hinterland and a foreign power laid claim to it.

Henry M. Stanley, made famous by his first visit to Africa in search of David Livingstone, came to the Congo later in the interest of the king of Belgium, and it was not long afterward that the land of Akelo was recognized by European powers as the Congo Free State with Leopold II, king of Belgium, as sovereign over it.

Again in 1887 Stanley entered Africa, this time to rescue Emin Pasha, the lost governor of Egypt's equatorial province. He reached the lower end of Lake Albert after 160 days of trekking through the vast Ituri forest. As he traveled from the coast to Stanleyville under the escort of the traitorous Arab slave trader, Tippu Tib, he found village after village abandoned because of a great famine. Apparently the famine was widespread, and it may well have been the one which changed the course of Akelo's life and brought her into the family of Moro Sheeba's paternal forebears.

The exact time of Akelo's birth is not known, but when the famine came she was possibly seven years old and her mother had two children who were younger than she was. In those painful days, the village Pa Dolo lay hot in the tropical sun, its grass as brown as the thatch which covered its beehive-shaped huts. But in spite of the long-continued drought, the gardens must be worked in the hope of rain and food. One day Akelo's mother strapped the youngest baby on her back and prepared to go to her garden. Akelo cried in protest and clung to her mother when she was bidden to remain in the village to mind the other child, but her mother was firm and made her stay behind.

Akelo was left alone in the village except for her small charge, for all the other villagers had gone away too. She continued to weep bitterly for her mother. It was thus that a stranger found her when he entered the deserted village Pa Dolo. He too was feeling the pinch of hunger, and, whatever his intended errand might have been, he saw before him the means of obtaining food.

"Why are you crying?" he asked Akelo.

"I want to go to the garden to my mother," she sobbed.

The stranger pretended great concern for the child. He would take her to her mother, he said, if she would stop crying. Akelo allowed him to carry her. Quickly he set out on one of the paths which led from the village Pa Dolo—but not toward the village gardens—and he kept on walking for many hours.

There must have been many misgivings in the little girl's heart as they left the familiar environs of her home village without coming upon her mother in the garden. Perhaps the glib stranger entertained her with captivating folk tales. Perhaps he kept her confidence by promises of plentiful food at their journey's end. Or perhaps she just stared silently at the strange new sights, too frightened to do anything but cling to him for protection. They traveled up and down small hills, crossed streams, and finally came to mountains. The rocky winding paths were steep, often with elephant grass on either side so tall and thick that it cut off all the breezes. One could not know where leopards might be sleeping in the rocky caves or what other dangers surrounded them. In those long-ago days it was not considered safe to go far from one's home village, so there seldom was any communication between the north and the south of Alurland. But when hungry one will dare any path, so the stranger pressed steadily on in his southward course.

At last they left the steep mountain trails and came out on a plain dotted here and there with hills. To the left of them was the escarpment leading down to Lake Albert. In the distance on the right towered another mountain range. Here there was food, for the plain was fertile. The stranger walked toward a village that stood on one of the hills. When he arrived, he found that the father of the village was one Bondo. To Bondo he described the hunger of the people of his home village. He explained that he was sore pressed and had brought his child in exchange for food.

No questions were asked in those days. It was a man's own affair if he wanted to sell his child for food. Bondo needed to consider the proposition from the standpoint of his own profit only. The fertile plain where he lived was unaffected by the famine. It would be no hardship to feed an extra mouth. Bondo may well have reasoned that there was much work to be done in his large village; that his wives needed someone to help them; that the child could take care of the babies, carry water from the stream, grind grain, frighten birds from the garden, and perform countless other small chores; that when she was old enough to be married, she would bring him wealth in sheep and goats if he chose to sell her out of his own family. At any rate, he was willing to bargain for her.

There probably was much palaver before the price was set at one bag of Kaffir corn and two bags of millet. Then Bondo's wives would have climbed into the granaries and handed out sufficient grain to fill three bags. Very likely the stranger had brought his own bags, made of the whole skins of bush bucks. He would have hooked the legs of the full bags on a stick and swung them over his shoulders to carry.

Now Akelo was the property of Bondo. Her captor took leave of the bewildered child with an explanation that her new owner did not hear.

"I am going to leave you here with my relatives," he said, "so that you can have food to eat."

Then he was off, weighted down with the bags of grain. Where he slept that night, or if he ever reached his village in safety, no one from Bondo's village ever knew.

Chapter 2

AKELO THE SLAVE GIRL

IN THE DAYS that followed the arrival of Akelo on Libi hill, Bondo learned much through questioning the child, for her indifference to the departure of her supposed father had made him realize that he had been deceived and that the man from whom he had bought her was not her father. He learned now that her real father's name was Ung'ona and that her home was in the faraway village Pa Dolo.

The purchase of little Akelo was not thought of as an unusual thing in those days—at the close of a century that was marked by the war being waged on slavery, Africa's "open sore" that had grieved the hearts of Livingstone and others as they beheld the terrible traffic in human beings. Yet slavery was not the business of the Arabs alone, although they carried the traffic to an excess of cruelty. It was practiced also among the Africans themselves. The buying and selling of slaves was carried on largely between the big chiefs or clans, but if an ordinary person desired to own a slave, there was no tribal law against it. Bondo, however, was no ordinary person. He came from a royal line.

Each evening Bondo and other village elders would sit around the *kadipo,* the place of daily gathering for the men, though women and children sometimes sat on the outer edge of the circle. The center of every village *kadipo* was its fire, in the soft glow of which as the evening shadows lengthened, the old men warmed up to their tales of long ago or the folklore of the tribe. When the embers died out in the dark, it was the signal for them to go to their huts to sleep. When the stories were especially fascinating, the little boys were wont to edge up close to the fire and surreptitiously pull the sticks away to make it die out sooner. Otherwise they would be sent off to sleep before the tales were finished.

It was the custom of the elders, as they sat around the *kadipo,* to rehearse to their sons the names and deeds of their ancestors. Thus tribal and family history was handed down by one generation to the next. Bondo could remember the names of his forefathers for nine generations back. They were a line of paramount chiefs, the earliest of whom had lived and ruled on the other side of Lake Albert in Uganda. According to tradition, Chief Kambo's son had crossed the lake in a canoe that was made of burnt clay and had settled on the Congo side in what came to be known as Mu-Kambo-land. The line of chiefs who had ruled in Uganda continued to rule this large section of the Alur tribe. When Bondo's grandfather had died, the throne of Mukamboland passed to his eldest son, and Bondo's father was an important person in the kingdom as brother to the ruling chief. Doubtless Bondo's sons and grandsons were reminded of this fact often around the *kadipo,* and it could not have been long before Akelo, squatting with the women in the outer circle, realized that she was slave to a royal family.

Bondo was a kind man, and everyone in Bondo's village was so kind to Akelo that, once the first pangs of homesickness were over, she adjusted herself to the thought of being a slave girl and was satisfied to live among them. She was a good child, obedient, and a steady worker. Every day she was faithful in the duties assigned her by Bondo's wives. She was considered very industrious because she would anticipate a need and do many menial tasks not assigned to her. As she grew older, she could dig a garden, and she also became a good cook. She went cheerfully about her work regardless of the large number of people for whom she was expected to cook, for it seemed no effort at all to her.

Bondo looked upon Akelo with great approval. Nor did she go unobserved by others outside the family. Many a father in the nearby villages would have been pleased to purchase the little slave girl for his son. But when they approached Bondo on the subject, he had the same answer for all of them.

"No, I will not sell her," they were told.

Akelo was ignorant of the fact that, ere she had been long in Bondo's village, Bondo had called the youngest of his four sons, whose name was Gem,[1] and had told him that when Akelo was old enough to be married he might have her for an additional wife. It was no dishonor to marry a slave girl. Wives were purchased to bear children for their husbands. The children did not belong to the mother, but to the father and his family. Bondo bought wives for his sons so they would bear sons and keep the family tree alive. If one wife did not bear a son, it would be necessary to purchase another wife who would. It was always the fault of the wife if she bore no children, or only daughters, though daughters of course were needful. With the wealth in sheep and goats and cows that he received for his daughters, the father of the village could buy wives for his sons. If Bondo had paid only grain for this slave girl, that was no affair.

Akelo might or might not have entered her teens when she was married to Gem. Since she was only a slave girl and had grown up in the village of the man whom she was to marry, she did not have the privilege of making the customary journey to her bridegroom's village, with the girls of her own village, to

[1]The "G" is hard as in "girl."

work in the garden of her future mother-in-law. Already for years she had worked in the gardens of Bondo's wives.

The other wedding festivities were observed, however. According to the custom, she spent the two days previous to her marriage proper in the wedding hut, which was the hut of Gem's brother. The village elder brought her out of this hut with her little finger tied to Gem's. Amid great hilarity and the blowing of his whistle, he "showed her the path." Gem led the way and Akelo followed, her finger still attached to Gem's, while a crowd of people came on behind them.

When the people had shown the couple several paths, Gem and Akelo were made to sit close together on the ground with their legs stretched out in front of them. Then the master of ceremonies killed a chicken over their outstretched legs. The chicken fell with its legs together and the people yelled with joy, for this was the assurance that Akelo would be a good wife and not run off to other men. Sometimes when this part of the ceremony was performed, the chicken would fall on its back with its legs separated. At such times there would be no rejoicing, only silence, for the people would know that the girl who was being married would run away from her husband and cause him much trouble and sorrow.

But Akelo's wedding was one of rejoicing only, and the falling of the chicken with its legs together must have been a foregone conclusion. Had not all the countryside been witness to the industry and obedience of the slave girl all the years that she had lived in Bondo's village? On the evening of her wedding day, the little slave bride was taken to her husband's hut, where she began a new life as Gem's possession, to be the mother of his children, one of whom was to be known and loved far and wide in the villages of Mukamboland of the Alurs.

Chapter 3

BORN INTO DARKNESS

THE FAVOR with which the slave girl had been regarded in the village of Bondo continued to rest upon her as the wife of Gem, for her first-born child was a son, always a cause of rejoicing in the clan. Akelo herself was quite satisfied with her lot. Her husband, though small of stature for a man, was of a good physique and surpassed all other men on the plain for work. He was a peace-loving man who would allow no discontent around him. Not only did his village relatives appreciate him, but his cousin the chief liked him because of his good influence and quiet disposition. He hated deceit and wanted affairs to be settled uprightly with nothing shady about them.

Gem was a husband to be proud of as he went about in his garb of antelope skin, which only those of royal lineage could wear, and the little bunches of twisted hair that had been rubbed with fat and red clay and the finely ground rock *upila,* until his whole head glistened with the white *upila.* What could be more to the credit of a woman of Alurland than to give so fine a husband a son to carry on his family tree and thus fulfill the purpose of her purchase? So Akelo nursed little Baru and went cheerfully about the multitudinous labors that fall to the lot of a wife and mother in her tribe. But this prosperity did not last through her married life. Sorrow soon began to "eat" her, for her next two babies died.

When Akelo gave birth to a fourth child, she thought of her two dead babies and named the little one Shanda, "I-have-suffered-for-nothing," for this one, too, would die. But baby Shanda did not die as her mother sadly anticipated. She lived and grew up to be the Moro Sheeba, who was destined to carry to the people of this very plain and all the surrounding country a message from the God they did not know and a Book of which they never had heard.

The village in which Shanda was born was not the village on Libi hill where her mother had been bought as a little girl and where she was married to Gem. Gem and his brother Keno had built a new village at the foot of Ugeu hill on the same fertile plain. Very likely the cause for the move had been the fear of death, for Bondo and his two oldest sons had died on Libi hill. When Akelo gave birth to Shanda, there were about twelve huts in the new village. Her Uncle Keno lived there with his wives, and another relative had attached himself and family to the village. There were also huts for her father's four wives—for he had inherited the wife of her Uncle Mugasa and the wife of her Uncle Rasham. It was his duty to beget sons of them in order to keep alive the names of his dead brothers. Consequently the first son to be born to him by each of these wives went by the name of the dead husband who was accounted as his father. When Shanda was born, her half brother Mugasa, who was to be very close to her throughout her lifetime, was a sturdy youth who lived in the hut with the other unmarried young men of the village. The junior Rasham came along late enough for her to be nursemaid to him.

Every known precaution was taken by her parents to insure the welfare of Shanda. To the women, who had come in to help her and were present at the birth, Akelo gave gifts of food to prevent their going blind. She put flour on their faces, after she had fulfilled her four days in the hut for the birth of a girl-child, and was brought out by the local master of such ceremonies. The master of ceremonies took her with the newborn babe to the stream so she could appease Adranga, the dreaded spirit of the stream. He showed her also the path to go for wood when he appeased the evil spirit of the mountain.

Akelo and the baby were given the medicine of *songwa* to drink in the hope that the mother would be able to keep her child. Gem bought a big seed called *litra* and had it tied on a string around Shanda's little neck to protect her head from sores. When a serious illness overtook the baby and he saw her thin and at the point of death, he gladly furnished a chicken and a goat that Akelo might sacrifice for her. Because Shanda recovered, the relatives gave the sacrifice credit for sparing her life. Anxiously Akelo awaited the cutting of her baby's first teeth, for the cutting of the upper ones first was a terrible omen and would require an immediate sacrifice. Great was her relief when she saw Shanda's lower teeth come through first.

Thus little Shanda began her life in the land of the Alurs. There was nothing to indicate for her a destiny different from that of any other girl-child of the tribe. She learned to walk and talk and play with the children of the family village, taking for granted her father's other wives and the endless precautions to avert the wrath of Jok,[1] his countless servant demons, and the spirits of her dead ancestors to all of whom her people attributed the power to bring prosperity or suffering to any one of them.

Shanda's home, like all the other huts in the village, was built in the shape of a beehive and thatched with grass that came right to the ground. A little passageway, like a tunnel,

[1]The Jok of the Alur is identified easily as the Satan of Scripture. The spirit beings under his control are referred to as "little Joks," although they have individual names many of which are known, such as Songwa, and Adranga, the spirit of the stream. The spirits of Jok are quite distinct from the spirits of the dead who also are worshiped.

led from its small door. In this passageway Shanda would keep the fires going for Akelo when she was cooking food, for that was the kitchen. Shanda considered it no hardship to have to stoop over in order to enter the passageway and go through that to the hut. Nor did she realize that the dark, windowless hut was a breeding place for sickness. The stench from the goats and sheep and chickens that slept in the hut with them did not bother her, for it never entered her mind that things could be different.

Mother Akelo was a good housekeeper as housekeepers went at that time. At least once a week she would "varnish" the floor with fresh cow dung to keep down the jiggers and chicken lice. By the time that Shanda was five, her mother had taught her how to mix the cow dung with water to the right consistency and help to smear it on the earthen floor. Soon she was old enough to help with many of the household tasks. She was an obedient, faithful child as her mother Akelo had been, and she inherited from both her parents the natural industry and the standards which were high for the time and place in which they lived.

When Akelo went to the nearby stream each morning and afternoon to carry water for cooking and the family baths, she would take Shanda along. When she was three or four years old, Akelo gave her a very tiny earthen pot and made her a circle mat with which to carry the pot on her head. It did not matter if most of the water splashed out coming home or if she stubbed her toe and dashed the little pot to pieces on the ground. Her efforts were repaid and at an early age, like all other Alur girls, she could walk gracefully carrying a pot of water on her head. She learned to put a few leaves in the water so it would not splash much. There was garden work too, and who was better fitted to teach Shanda to handle a cultivating hoe, to weed, and to dig than her mother, Akelo?

For the first ten years of her life, Shanda was not cumbered with clothes. So long as she had a string around her waist, she was considered dressed. But how shocked her elders would have been if a girl dared to appear in public without the necessary string! The child must have admired the finely woven iron-chain skirt which her mother wore, a skirt which fitted over each hip, meeting in the front but not completely covering the back, and decorated with beads and cowrie shells.

Sometimes when it was very hot or the work was slack in the gardens, Akelo would use the time to shave Shanda's head, making interesting designs or leaving a tuft or two of hair on her head. The village women shaved one another's heads in designs too. Some of the younger men, instead of decorating their hair with red clay and white *upila* rock, chose to shave their heads also, but never in a feminine design.

The Alur had many ornaments with which to enhance their beauty. Shanda wore a wire bracelet that was wound around and around her arm starting at the wrist and going up to her elbow. Some of the girls wore them on their legs as well. They also had bracelets made from heavy ore. If they wore a number of these on their ankles and wrists, they would make a lot of noise and attract attention when they danced. Both men and women wore large iron necklaces. Shanda had a small one which she wore even as a little girl. She also had rings in her lips and ears made from brass which Uganda Africans had obtained from the Indians and brought across the lake to trade for food.

After Shanda had gotten her second teeth, the old women of the village held her down while she went through the ordeal of having her two lower front teeth gouged out. This was necessary for every Alur. The older girls and boys had the design of the tribe cut on their foreheads, stomachs, and backs, but Shanda was still too young for that. It was a painful process as the pattern was cut with a crude knife and a mixture of red clay and fat placed under the cut skin. But the raised design made by the welts when they healed was much admired.

For several years Shanda carried on her leg a bad sore which would not heal. The people in the village said that the relatives of Shanda's mother were causing the sore, so they caught a goat, spit upon it, and said,

"Take this sore and go away with it so that the leg of our child may heal."

Many in the family had these stubborn sores and much of their wealth was paid to the witch doctors in the hope that they might receive healing. There was no one in those days to explain to Shanda or her relatives that the sores were caused by yaws, how contagious the disease was, or how it might be treated, so they coped with sicknesses in the only way they knew.

Peeking around the granaries on certain occasions, Shanda could watch her father Gem with the other village elders sacrificing over the *abila* sticks. These were small sticks pounded into the ground in front of Gem's hut so that the spirit of his dead father, Bondo, would rest upon it. His spirit would watch over Gem's village and keep his people well. Shanda saw that her father was a very religious man, and he spoke to the spirit of the dead with great reverence as he and the elders rubbed the liver and poured the blood of sacrificial animals over these sticks. But often there was fear that they had displeased the spirit of Bondo and that was the reason for many of their sicknesses and sores. It was but one of the many fears which cast their constant shadows over the sensitive soul of the keen-minded little girl who was growing up in the village at the foot of Ugeu hill.

A baby brother had been born while Shanda was still very small, but he lived only a short time. When the next little one was expected, her mother was not well. Everyone in the village was sure that Adranga, the evil spirit of the stream, was causing the sickness, so Akelo must resort to sacrifice again. She placed

The author with six of the first overseers of *Monkwenda*

A Sunday service out of doors at Awasi, when the material was being gathered for the book

Upio p'Ajika (center), Pilipili's brother Musasi (in sweater), and another brother

Simon Ugwoko (Awasi evangelist-teacher) and his family

Yohana Ukumu, now chief of Mukamboland

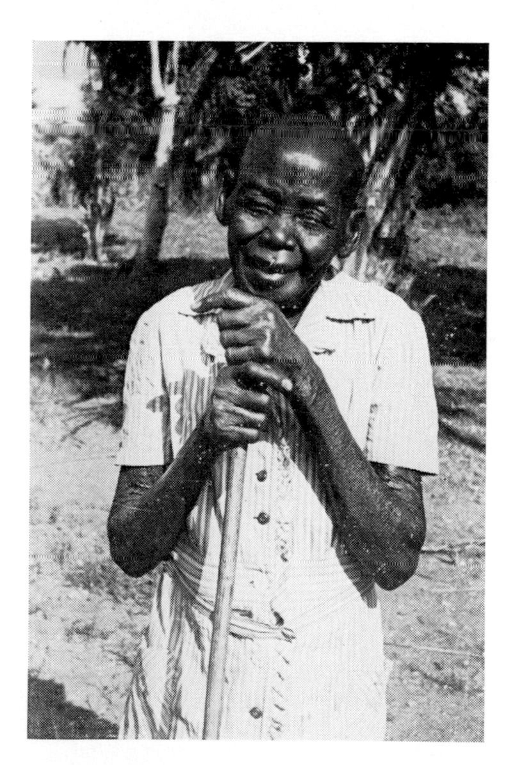

Old Maria
who took care
of Sheeba's family
during her last illness

Awasi church and schoolhouse on the site of Moro's old hut

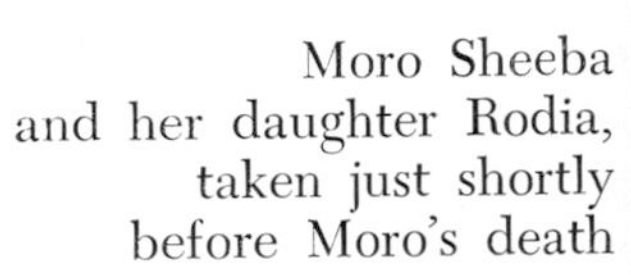

Moro Sheeba
and her daughter Rodia,
taken just shortly
before Moro's death

egg and flour and red clay on the edge of the stream for Adranga, confident that the child would be born safely because she had "paid the stream."

When the little girl was born she was called Nyatto, "the daughter of death," because Akelo had saved her child from the clutches of death by appeasing Adranga. But Nyatto was a frail little baby and often ill. Each time she became sick, Shanda's father went to call on the prophet. He would take a gift of a chicken or flour or grain or a hoe and ask the prophet to pray to the spirits of the dead to show him what to do. When the old prophet had received Gem, he would take a stick and chant as he thumped it up and down on the ground, all the time listening closely.

"It is the mother of the stream that is causing the sickness," he announced to Gem on one of these occasions. "You must appease it with a sacrifice."

Gem came home and selected a sheep from his flock, which he tied at the door of the hut in which Akelo was sitting with little Nyatto. When Won Adranga, the "father" of Adranga, who was the big witch doctor of the stream, arrived, Akelo dashed out of the hut with baby Nyatto in her arms and vines tied around her head. She seized the sheep and put it on her shoulders. Holding it around her neck by its feet, she ran with it and her baby to the stream. The Won Adranga, spear in hand, dashed after her, with the old men and women following.

At the stream Akelo cast herself and baby and sheep into the water in the sight of the excited crowd. Won Adranga snatched the baby and threw his spear into the stream to pierce the death that was working the child. Then he rescued the sheep and killed it on the bank so that its blood ran into the stream as an offering to Adranga. When the meat was cooked, the old men and women were allowed to eat it because they had sacrificed to Adranga before. Only then did the Won Adranga send Akelo back into the village with her baby in expectation that the child would get well.

Shanda would not have been permitted to witness the ceremony at the stream but, tiny though she was, she could not have been unaffected by the transient hope it afforded or the pathos of the customary wail which broke from her mother's lips a few days later,

"*Aka-yo! Aka!* (My child has really died. What will I do? What will I hold in my arms?) *Aka! Aka! Aka!*"

Little Nyatto was dead. The men of the village dug a deep hole in their yard, wrapped the little body, and lowered it into the grave. They filled in the dirt and stomped upon it. There was no attempt to shield little Shanda or any of her small cousins, her village brothers and sisters, from the stark reality of death. They were present when the babies entered the world, and they looked without comfort on death's visit to their village, their little hearts chilled by the hopeless wail of the bereaved mother,

"What will I hold in my arms? *Aka! Aka! Aka!*"

Chapter 4

THE BIRTH OF THE LITTLE DEVILS

SHANDA'S FAITH in the power of the witch doctors must have been shaken again and again. Her mother bore four more children to Gem in quick succession after the death of little Nyatto. As each one sickened, she saw her father give goats, sheep, chickens, and hoes to the witch doctors, but all the babies died. Then a worse tragedy struck their home. If Shanda was present, as undoubtedly she was, she would have been pushed abruptly out of her mother's hut as the women who were attending Akelo at another childbirth rushed out of the hut in fright. Little devils were being born! Jok had created two babies, and demons lived in them! Who wanted to endanger their lives by staying on the scene?

If Akelo had not been a slave girl, a messenger would have been dispatched immediately to her home village with a white chicken. He would have thrown the chicken at the door of Akelo's father's hut and cursed her parents because their daughter had borne little devils. Then he would have run away. The parents would have given him chase, and if they had succeeded in catching him, his relatives would have had to bring a goat to redeem him. But Akelo's parents were not known, so no messenger could be sent to them. Others in the village had to take their place when they "tied Jok" on the babies. They tied little shells and beads on their bodies on a string, and they called them Upio and Udongo, the names always given by the Alur to boy-baby devils.

There was much cursing over the birth of Upio and Udongo. Akelo cursed Gem. Gem cursed Akelo. They both cursed everyone in the village, and the villagers all cursed them and the parents that bore Akelo. For a whole moon Shanda could not live with her mother or the babies, and she never could live in that hut again. Was it not cursed because little devils had been born in it? Shanda had been growing up with the sound of cursing about her every day, but never had the cursing been so vehement or so constant as now that her mother had given birth to two babies instead of one.

Under no circumstances could the mother of little devils come out of the hut where they were born until a whole moon had passed, nor could any of the trash be carried out during that time. Shanda was taken into the hut of one of Gem's other wives to sleep and eat until her own mother could care for her again. The Wang'u Jok, the "grandmother" of Satan, spent the moon in the hut with Akelo and the little devils. She had powerful medicine which she blew around the mother and the babies. She had charms also which she tied on the little devils, and the cursing continued throughout the month.

The priest of the mountains was called. He and the Wang'u Jok killed a sheep and the babies had to lie on its skin. Before long one of the babies died. Its little body was placed in an earthen pot and the mouth of the pot was sealed with clay. This pot stayed inside the hut beside two other double-mouthed clay pots, one belonging to each twin, which contained the refuse at the time of their birth. None of the pots could be brought outside until the month's ceremonies all had been performed. Nor was any sweeping of the hut permitted, so the pile of refuse and ashes grew very large. At the end of the month, some of Gem's relatives, acting the part of Akelo's parents, demanded of Gem and the others,

"You take our child out of the hut. The month is finished. She has lived in the trash long enough."

Then Gem, as the father of the twins, sent a goat to Akelo's acting parents and they came to take the slave-girl wife out of the hut. They brought a sheep and different kinds of grain and other food. Gem called upon one of the elders of the village to help him bring out the mother and the remaining twin. They did not dare to bring them out by the doorway, for they would surely die if this was done, so the village elder made a hole in the back of the hut.

When the hole was made, the Wang'u Jok came out of it, followed by Shanda's mother with the living twin, then the three earthen pots, one of which contained the body of the other twin. All of the trash was swept out at the hole as well. The Wang'u Jok led the procession to a shady tree, blowing medicine right and left from her open hand as they went down the path. She was appeasing the evil spirits so they would spare the lives of the mother and the other babe. Under the tree, they made three holes in the ground just deep enough to bury the bottoms of the earthen pots, and left them there. Then, still blowing her medicine, the Wang'u Jok led them back to the village and to the place of sacrifice. There they killed a sheep and the skin of it was saved to be made into a carrying strap for the living child. The skin for the child who died was given to the mother to sit on.

When these ceremonies were concluded, the people encompassed the village and danced. After they had encircled the village twice, Akelo was taken to the new hut which they had been building for her during the month of her imprisonment. To use even the poles or any other part of the old hut would have meant certain death, so the old hut was left to rot. After

Gem had given a bull for meat for the relatives who had come to bring Akelo out of the hut, all the people separated and returned to their various villages. Now Shanda was permitted to live with her mother again.

Sorrow followed on sorrow in the village of Gem, for soon the other twin died. Of the twelve children which Akelo had borne only Baru, her first-born, and Shanda were left. She was under many curses for the rest of her life because she had given birth to little devils. Shanda, with her sensitive nature, always grieved to see her mother so. How had they failed in appeasing the evil spirits and the spirits of the dead? Gem and Akelo had tried always to do what was right. They were faithful in performing all their duties of worship and sacrifice, but perhaps they had not known the way of the spirits and were displeasing them. Yet they knew of no other way, so there was nothing to do but to keep right on seeking to placate them lest Baru and Shanda be taken from them as their other children had been.

Chapter 5

WAR FOR THE THRONE OF MUKAMBOLAND

DURING THE EARLY YEARS of Shanda's life the outside world had become conscious of the rich inland country where she lived. The environs of Lake Albert already had been visited by a succession of white foreigners, some of whom had left a trail of panic and bloodshed behind them. It was little wonder that when the Belgians first came into this part of the Congo to set up their government centers, they were met with suspicion and distrust.

There had been great fear in the village of Gem when the Belgian safari passed through, for Gem and his family had not forgotten the man, an Arab by the name of Alober, who had marched this way long ago and one of whose soldiers had killed Shanda's two cousins, the children of her Uncle Rasham. It had been a great relief to the villagers when they had seen the Belgians march on without any disturbance to set up their headquarters near the lake to the north. Now the benign King Albert I was on the throne, and the ruling country was granting to the tribal chiefs much of their original authority.

However, panic gripped the peaceful countryside again in the spring of 1912, when Shanda was about ten years old. Old grievances over the throne of Mukamboland had come to a head. The government post had been moved inland to Mahagi in the district from which Akelo had been stolen as a child. Across the nearby border of Uganda dwelt a banished brother of the ruling chief. Bent on getting back to his own country and ruling as chief, he was laying plans to this end when someone shot an arrow through his side at night. Sure that the reigning chief had sent the arrow, he and his son, Katto, determined to have revenge. Accordingly, Katto went to the government post and made many false accusations against his uncle, the chief. So successfully did he present his case that a white officer and many African soldiers were sent to deal with the chief by force.

As soon as the white man arrived in the vicinity, the chief sent him food for himself and his soldiers. The white man, realizing that he would not have done this had he wanted to fight, called him to come out for a talk. The chief refused.

"You have come with Katto," he said, "the son of my brother who has become my enemy. I dare not come out to see you."

When the true situation dawned on him, the Belgian officer ordered Katto back to Uganda, telling him it was he who was the father of this war. Instead of obeying the government official, Katto collected his followers and made a surprise attack on the chief's village. Before anyone could stop them, they tore down the tall elephant-grass enclosure around the village, entered the chief's hut and took possession of his chair, the symbol of the kingdom, and began to snatch his bows from the wall. The sudden cry of alarm alerted the chief's loyal subjects, who seized their weapons and came running to his rescue.

Back in the village of Gem, Shanda's half brother Mugasa, some sixteen years her senior, and other men of their village rushed off with their bows and arrows and spears to defend the kingdom of their chief. Her mother Akelo and the other women hung around their huts that day until the uproar of the fighting came too close. Then they scampered off to the tall grass with their children. There young Shanda hid with her playmates until it was safe to go home.

It was well that the women kept off the paths and hid in the tall grass, for when the white man saw that war was inevitable, he started to retreat with his soldiers, taking Katto with him. As they walked, the angry Katto would shoot at anyone he chose, and the people all along the way kept answering the challenge by shooting back. Mugasa and his fellow villagers knew that the path of retreat, with this wild shooting, would take the soldiers right through the village of Gem, so they hurried ahead to be ready to defend their families.

"The white man is very tough. The arrow will not go through him," a number of men remarked to Mugasa that day.

"Is it really true that the white man is so tough that an arrow cannot go through him?" Mugasa tossed the thought over and over in his mind as he hid behind a big anthill to await the coming of the soldiers. "I would like to see if it is really true."

He did not have long to wait. As the white man passed, Mugasa pulled back his bowstring and let an arrow fly. It skimmed across the white man's forehead and knocked off his sun helmet. Immediately the white man aimed his gun at the anthill and shot four times, demolishing the anthill. Mugasa was not wondering now if the white man was tough. He was running for another shelter. No sooner had he hidden behind a big rock than four of the white man's soldiers slipped up behind him and began to shoot. Mugasa was agile enough to dodge so that the shells fell on the rock instead of on him, but the soldiers gave him chase, along with the other men of Gem's village. They got close enough to take away Mugasa's spear and the spear and bow of his brother, yet he and his fellow villagers managed to escape under cover of the cloud of smoke from the soldiers' guns.

The soldiers passed on till they came to another hill on the fertile plain where they fought all day. It was there that another relative of Shanda's, a man by the name of Udubre, made bold to aim at the white man's African bodyguard, and the arrow went through his heart and back. The bodyguard fell on his back, still holding the gun in his hand.

"Get the gun! Get the gun!" yelled Udubre's companions.

Not knowing the wisdom of the white man's gun or that it was aimed at him, poor Udubre ran toward the fallen bodyguard and seized the gun by the barrel. In his dying moment, the bodyguard drew the trigger and split Udubre's head open.

Before returning to Mahagi post, the white man and his soldiers buried the bodyguard on the hill where he had fought. But as soon as they had gone, the local people, worked up to a frenzy, dug up the corpse of the bodyguard. They placed it upon a big stack of wood, piled more wood on top of it, then lit a fire and burned it in revenge for the death of Udubre. When the news of this reached the government post, two officers and a large army of black soldiers were sent back to Mukamboland.

Shanda and her brother Mugasa were not in Gem's village when the soldiers returned. They had been taken with other relatives many miles away across a treacherous river and up into the mountains. Later when they came home to their fertile plain, they found that it had been the scene of much bloodshed for the soldiers had killed many people. One woman in Gem's own village had lost her life at their hands.

The men, as they sat once more on the big stones that formed their village *kadipo* and discussed the recent events, did not blame the Belgians for the war. None of the people in Mukamboland blamed the white man. They blamed the chief's banished brother and his son for deceiving the white man. And after that there was no more war with the government.

Chapter 6

BETROTHED

AMONG THE PORTERS who carried the white man's loads, when he went to settle the trouble over the throne of Mukamboland, was a husky young man with full cheeks, to whom his friends had given the name of Pilipili, or Pepper, because he was light in color like their pepper. It could easily have been on this very trip, when the white man led his soldiers through her father's village, that Pilipili was attracted to Shanda and determined to send his relatives to bargain for her. He may have stopped at his home village on the way back to Mahagi post and told his brother Musasi about her, for it was soon after this that the negotiations for Shanda began.

It was a long time since Pilipili had lived at home in Awasi. His father had died before he was born and his mother had died when he was a little herdboy of perhaps ten years. So when he grew older he had left home and gone to live near the government post with his friend, Uceng', who was the head of a village there. It was not always safe to live among strangers so far from one's own village, for one never knew when someone in the village might say,

"*Eh,* this is a stranger. Let us kill him and get rid of him."

But if the stranger had become the blood friend of someone in the village, no one would dare to touch him, for he would have the protection of his friend. So Pilipili and Uceng' had become blood friends. Pilipili had cut his side, put some of the blood in a soggy bit of dough, and placed it in Uceng's mouth for him to eat. Then Uceng' had done the same for Pilipili and they had sworn that they would not do badly to one another. Thus Pilipili could trust Uceng', and it was easy to find remunerative work so near the government post.

Even if he had been living at home, Pilipili would not have initiated the proceedings to obtain a wife for himself. Because his father was dead, it fell to the lot of his older brother to do this for him. So Musasi set out for the village of Gem. All unknown to Shanda, this stranger visited her father and obtained his permission to start payment on her as Pilipili's future wife. It was not considered necessary, even by as kind a father as Gem, to consult little girls when marriage negotiations were made. It would take time, perhaps several years, to get together sufficient goats, cloth, hoes, and other wealth to warrant Pilipili's family claiming her as their property, but at least Gem was satisfied with the deal, and Musasi went home to report the success of his errand. Then it was up to Pilipili and the rest of the family to procure the necessary wealth.

Custom dictated that Pilipili should come himself with Musasi at the time that the first payment of goats was made, and then, if not before, Shanda must have learned that she was betrothed. Thereafter, Musasi and his village brothers visited Gem's village from time to time to make further payments on her. Her village sisters never thought of refusing when they were sent to sleep in the huts with these visiting boys from Pilipili's village. That was always done.

It was after the goats of Pilipili had begun to arrive in Gem's village and Shanda was developing into young womanhood that she received her "praise" name. The name which her mother had given her at birth was only for childhood. Now she must have a new name by which she would be known throughout her adult life. According to the custom, this name was bestowed upon her, not by her parents, but by her girl playmates who had received their own "praise" names already. They chose to call her Moro, a name frequently given to a girl who was slight in build and more brown than black in color. From then on she was spoken of no longer as Shanda but addressed by her "praise" name, Moro.

Not long after she had received her "praise" name, Moro became aware that her father intended to permit the customary visit to her future husband's village. Had his people not brought twenty goats, a yard of cloth, a hoe, beads, and a big bunch of dried fish? Had they not just killed a male goat and brought it to Moro's mother to remind Gem and Akelo that they had paid a large amount of their daughter's dowry? Of course they must bring at least fifteen more goats, besides a cloth for Moro, before they could claim her permanently, but Gem was ready to let her visit her husband's village, a village that seemed very far away to the little bride-to-be. Moreover, Moro did not want Pilipili for a husband.

"He is old and has big fat cheeks," she said derisively.

Moro pleaded with her father not to send her to Pilipili's village, and for a time he was lenient with her. But Pilipili's relatives were not to be put off. When they saw that Gem did not send her, they took the matter to the chief. Then Moro was compelled to go.

No bride-to-be ever made the preliminary trip to visit her future in-laws alone, so Moro was accompanied by a number of her village sisters, young girls of her family who went along to show her the path and to carry her few possessions. Together they followed the narrow path through the tall elephant grass and made their way to Awasi. Pilipili, of course, was not there. He was working away up near the Uganda border. But Pilipili's aunt, who acted in the place of his mother, welcomed her and her friends. It was not too hard for Moro to be among strangers as long as her village sisters were with her, but they could stay only a few days, for that was all the custom would allow. When it was time for them to leave, she accompanied them a short distance down the path, bade them good-by, and returned to find all eyes upon her.

Moro's future in-laws were anxious to know what kind of a wife their son was getting. Promptly they undertook to train her in the ways of their family. From early morning until late in the afternoon she worked in the garden. At first she had had the help of her village sisters, but when they left she had to do it alone. When she came back to the village, she would eat food that was prepared by her "aunt-in-law." Not until she had been duly initiated could she cook food in her husband's village. There were other things which she must do first.

Then came the day when Pilipili's brother Musasi announced that he was taking her to her husband. Every fiber of her small body shrank from this next step, but she knew that she had to go. Because her father had received wealth on her, Pilipili had a right to this visit. So Moro stumbled unwillingly after Musasi along the crooked stony path which led northward up a steep mountain, over a mountain range, and onto a plain to the village of Cobo, where Pilipili lived with his friend Uceng' and worked as a soldier in the village of the subchief.

The wife of Uceng' received Pilipili's bride-to-be for him, but Moro was very unhappy there. She did not like Pilipili and she did not want to be married to him. During the two months of her stay with him she kept begging to be sent back to Awasi, secretly hoping that from there she could find her way back to the village of her father. Finally Pilipili, realizing that she was little more than a child and thinking that his family might be able to manage her, consented to her return to his home village.

Having arrived at Awasi, Moro began to plead with Pilipili's family to let her go home to her father's village. They agreed, but first Musasi went out to the flock to pick out a goat, which he killed for her before she left. She ate the meat which was served to her and carried the two hind legs home. Quickly she slipped back into her niche in the family of Gem, relieved that the visit was over. How wonderful it was to be near her mother, her father, her much-admired big brother Mugasa, and her many other village relatives! Gladly would she have stayed with them always—and it is certain that she was in no hurry to see Pilipili's family complete the payment of her dowry so they could take her away for good.

Chapter 7

ONE STRONGER THAN JOK

WHEN MORO RETURNED from her prolonged visit to Pilipili, she found a new spirit house inside her mother's hut. Akelo and others had been ill. The old prophet had said that their sickness was caused by an evil spirit and that Akelo must build a little hut for him inside her own and worship him there until he revealed his name. Undoubtedly Moro joined her mother when she made the daily offering of millet flour before this miniature hut and prayed to the spirit, whom she knew only as Amung', the silent one.

"I am giving you just a little taste, a suggestion of something better that I will be giving you. Give health to all in this hut," she would tell him respectfully.

Later, when the "something better," an offering of beer, was proffered, they would blow flour on the members of the household, saying as they did so,

"May your body be in health. May your body be in health."

But when Akelo's health continued to fail, she determined to become possessed by the silent spirit Amung'. The witch doctor and many old men and old women previously possessed by evil spirits gathered in her hut for the ceremony. All others, including Moro, were excluded. After a goat had been sacrificed and its skin wrapped around Akelo, the old women held her in their midst while they swayed and danced and chanted.

"What is your name, Jok?" they called repeatedly to the silent spirit.

In due time Akelo's eyes began to bulge, and a voice that was not hers answered through her,

"My name is Ukok."

Now that they knew his name, the people lost no time in killing another goat and initiating the ceremonies to move Ukok's little hut outside. They had all too vivid memories of how Moro's Aunt Abome, the wife of her Uncle Rasham, had gone out of her mind and been killed by an evil spirit whose hut she refused to move outside after he had revealed his name. They wanted to make sure that Akelo was not overtaken by a similar fate.

The split entrails of the sacrificial animal, after they had been dried for two days on Akelo's head, were folded up and sewed tightly into a small piece of bark cloth with a few grains of semsem, beans, and millet, trimmings from Akelo's fingernails, and a bit of her hair. This charm, called *ngisa,* was tied around Akelo's head before the witch doctor brought her out of her hut. Then she was taken to the tall grass to have her body decorated with white ashes. Upon her return to the village amid many welcoming overtures from the villagers, Ukok's hut was removed from her hut and placed outside with the other spirit huts, followed by dancing and ceremonial feasting.

As the witch doctor and the old men and women returned to their respective villages, Akelo was warned not to shave the hair of her head or to sleep on a bed. Night after night for weeks and then months, Moro had to see her mother sleeping on the bare dirt floor, while her woolly hair grew so long that it was hard to keep the lice out of it. Finally it was in order for her to call the witch doctor again to shave her head, which he did for the price of a hoe. Then he blew medicine on her bed and addressed the spirit by whom she had been possessed,

"Ukok, let this person be in good health. Today this person

is coming back to sleep on her bed. Sickness must not come near her again."

Now Akelo had been possessed by two evil spirits, Ukok and Kapirapira. She was very faithful in worshiping both of them and in bringing them gifts, yet her health did not improve. Moro did all she could to help her mother, but she must have wondered often why her mother's gods did not reward her devotion or answer her fervent prayers. Was Moro's mind being prepared to think favorably of a new doctrine that was just beginning to reach the ears of the Alur?

The very day that the Belgian officials and their soldiers had been in camp at Mahagi Port, on their way to settle the disturbance over the throne of Mukamboland, a party of white strangers had stepped out of a large boat on the western shore of Lake Albert and moved into the country of the Alurs, with all their foreign paraphernalia for living. For several months they had stayed in the neighborhood of Mahagi Port. One of their men had made a strong hut out of rocks on Api hill, but evidently the strangers were not content to stay there, for the men began to walk in different parts of the country, looking for a place to settle. Apparently they had been impressed by the big mountain, Kasengu, which the people of Moro's village could see silhouetted against the sky in the distance if they looked across their plain and beyond the top of a steep escarpment. There the strangers had cut down the elephant grass and built huts for themselves. There were four men, four women, and three little children.

These white men and women, telling of a strange God, were making safaris into all the country around Kasengu. They had even descended the great mountains and visited some of the villages on the plain. They were singing to everyone about a certain Jesus who loved everybody, and their faces looked happy as they talked about a God of love who was stronger than Jok. These strangers with the happy faces were kind to the

Alur and did many things to help them, but their teachings were regarded for the most part with suspicion.

The villages in Mukambo buzzed with excitement when one of the white men climbed Ara, the highest hill on the plain and not far from the village of Gem, and began to build a hut in which to live. Just before this, the paramount chief of Mukambo, to whom Moro and her family were related, had been seen with three of the men from Kasengu. It developed that the great chief had stopped at Kasengu with his village elders and his porters on his way home from the government post several months before. In appreciation of the interest shown in the welfare of his people, the chief had expressed a desire to have someone come to teach the people in his territory. Thus the white man had come to live at Ara at the invitation of the chief, so the people would have to respect him. However, they kept him under close observation lest their chief had been deceived.

The white man began to visit the people in their villages, with a reception that varied from place to place. In Gem's village, the people were polite to him, although the elders were annoyed that he tried to interest them in another God. Already it was taking everything that Gem had to appease all the evil spirits with which he had to deal. He did not want to add any more to their number. This man and his friends at Kasengu also had strange ideas about the *jajoks,* the old men or women witches to whom was attributed power to inflict sickness and death. The *jajoks* were dangerous to have around. They must be chased from their villages or even burned to death. Every little while, however, one would hear that a *jajok* had been rescued by the white men and actually taken to live at Kasengu for protection! Once one of the men came all the way to Mukamboland to the chief's village looking for a *jajok,* but he did not find her.

After two years the white man went away from Ara and no

one lived there for about six months. During this time, the paramount chief was put in jail by the Belgians for burning a *jajok,* and the kingdom was given to his brother, Abok. Chief Abok was ruling Mukamboland when the next *bwana*[1] appeared on Ara hill, followed shortly by two white *madamos*[2] one of whom was his wife. Chief Abok took a favorable attitude toward these foreign teachers and was willing to arrange for the building of a school on Ara. Then the government officials told Chief Abok that he must send some of his children to Ara to learn the wisdom of reading and writing so that they could help him in ruling his kingdom well. Abok sent two of his sons. Children of the subchiefs were called too, so five little boys of royal blood went to live on Ara. There Chief Abok's son, Ukumu, became a houseboy to one of the *madamos,* and it was not long before he became a believer in the white man's God.

By this time Moro was at least fifteen years old, a slender attractive girl of light complexion, who had watched apprehensively as Musasi had visited her village a number of times bringing goats and finally a cloth for her. She knew that it could not be long now before her father would have to let her go to live with Pilipili as his wife, for it was quite evident that his relatives had finished paying all the required wealth for her. But Moro did not want to be his wife now any more than when she had first made fun of his fat cheeks, or begged to be sent home when she had visited him.

At the same time crops were beginning to fail in all the surrounding country. Moro and her relatives knew what it was to go to bed hungry, but they struggled on with their gardens, hoping that they could harvest sufficient food to keep themselves alive. This too was a puzzle to Moro. Had not her father al-

[1]A title commonly given to white men throughout East and Central Africa. It is used alone or followed by the person's surname.

[2]In Belgian territory, *madamo* is the feminine counterpart of *bwana,* and was applied to both married and single women.

ways given of the first fruits of his gardens to Jok? Why was the great evil spirit treating her father in this way? She could not understand why the God of the people on Ara was more powerful than the great evil spirit, but Chief Abok's son, Ukumu, her relative, had informed them that the true God was helping them well. They planted gardens of potatoes on Ara, and the God to whom they had learned to pray made them ripen. They were not hungry on Ara hill. The *bwana* there was even getting food from some place else and was distributing it to the hungry people of the plain. More wondered if it could be that his God was more powerful than Jok whom her father worshiped.

When the two lady missionaries from Ara began to make frequent visits to Gem's village, Moro listened eagerly to what they had to say. Having seen her mother suffer, in spite of all the sacrifices to the evil spirits with which she had been possessed, and having watched her father dutifully lead his family and village in worshiping Jok and the spirits of the dead without receiving any help, she was ready to hear more about the new God who, even now, was supplying the needs of the black people who had put their trust in Him.

One day the lady missionary, who was not married, came through Moro's village calling the girls to go to Ara to be with her. There she would teach them more about her God, who she said was the true God, and there she could teach them how to read and write, even as Ukumu and the other boys were learning to do. She approached Moro and asked her if she would return to Ara with her. It may have been a wavering faith in the gods of Gem and Akelo, or it may have been that she saw a temporary escape from the impending claims of Pilipili, or perhaps it was a deep longing in her liver[3] to know

[3]In Alurland the liver, not the heart, is believed to be the seat of the emotions. Ukumu and others who accepted the new God "gave their livers to Jesus."

the God of love that impelled Moro to agree. What her parents thought of her venture is not known, but apparently they did not try to stop her as she followed the missionary to her home.

Chapter 8

THE PATH OF THE WHITE MAN'S GOD

It was a strange new world in which Moro found herself at Ara. Upon her arrival she was installed as cook in her missionary's kitchen. It was an honor to be given this position, so Moro did her best to please the *madamo.* She knew how to build a good fire, but she found a bewildering assortment of queer utensils with which to do her work, and even a white person's way of boiling water was different from the way her mother had taught her to do it. Yet, notwithstanding the problems involved, little by little Moro learned the art of cooking the foreign food.

Her clothes were different too. In the village she and the other girls had gathered soft leaves to make fresh garments every day. The smaller girls wore leaves only in the back, tied to the strings around their waists. The older girls wove the leaves together and wore them in front as well as in the back, as their mothers did—for the little chain skirts which Akelo used to wear were no longer in vogue. Moro had not been satisfied until she had obtained an *uposho* also. Made from strings of bark cloth or roots of the *agu* tree, and hung from the waistline behind, this accessory looked much like a horse's tail. Moro had looked forward to the day when she would be old enough to make her *uposho* long, reaching nearly to the ground, as some of the important older women were doing. But now her *uposho* was gone, and she wore a large piece of cloth fastened under her arms or sometimes a simple cotton dress, although she still clung to her bunch of leaves because she felt undressed without them. She learned how to wash this new clothing and make it clean again when it became soiled, for it could not be thrown away after a day's use.

The best of all Moro's new experiences, however, was that of going every day to the little mud and thatch schoolhouse to learn the lessons which the missionary lady had promised to teach her. She watched intently as the teacher would hold before the class a card on which a black mark had been printed and tell what it was.

"M," the class would repeat its name.

"Kendo" (again), the teacher would say with a smile.

"M."

"Kendo!"

"M."

"Kendo!"

"M."

The drill would continue with different marks until everyone was sure of their meaning. Moro joined the other girls and boys as they called out the letters and responded lustily after every *kendo.* In time she saw the marks put together to make the words of her mother tongue. At the end of every three months, those who knew their lessons well passed into a higher class, and then there was a month without any school. Moro never failed to pass. In fact she learned so quickly that by the end of the second three-month period, when she had been taught all the vowels and consonants, she could read parts of the Book of God which had been translated into her language. Soon after that she was reading fluently, with ability to understand what she read.

While Moro was eager to read and write, the happiest part

of each school session was when the missionary would tell more about the true God and about His Son. As she listened day by day many things became clear to her.

God loved her very much, but she was a sinner before Him. She had been born that way. Everyone was born that way because the first man and woman, who were the father and mother of all the people in the world, had rebelled against the true God when they were tempted by Jok to disobey Him. Ever since then, Jok had been deceiving people into following him and his evil spirits instead of God.

God could not forgive people and bless them again without a powerful sacrifice, so He had sent His Son to become a man and live on the earth and then to die on a cross for the sins of everyone in the whole world, even for the Alur who had not heard about Him. God's Son, who was called Jesus, became alive again and now He wanted to come into the hearts of people who would believe on Him so that He could wash away their sins in His blood. Then, when they finished their journey on earth, He would take them to live with Him always in a wonderful place called Heaven, where they never could be sick or sad any more. Everyone who did not believe on Jesus and worship the true God through Him would have to be punished forever with Jok and his evil spirits.

Moro knew that she was hearing the truth, and when she "turned her liver to Jesus," the change that took place inside was greater than all the outside changes which had come to her since she had lived on Ara. She was so happy that she wanted to tell all her relatives so that they could believe on Jesus and be protected by Him from Jok and his servant demons. How she drank in all that she was taught concerning the walk of one who has put her trust in the Son of God!

She lost her fear of the evil spirits and had no more faith in heathen charms. By reading the Book of God and listening to her teachers, she learned to see that which was wrong in the customs of her people and to forsake all that did not please the true God. She learned that one who had believed in Jesus should not marry one who is not a believer. Then how could she marry Pilipili? He was not a believer. She would sin against God if she married him now. She would pray to God and ask Him to help her.

On Sundays, after the special services for worshiping God were over, the children and young people who lived nearby were allowed to go home to visit their relatives. One Sunday afternoon when Moro was returning from her home to the mission station, some men jumped out of the tall grass beside the path to grab her. Like a flash Moro was off down the path and into the tall grass, for she recognized them as men from Pilipili's village.

"You belong to us," they called after her. "We have finished to pay all the wealth on you. Your parents say you are to go with us."

The men soon caught up with her and laid hands on her to take her with them by force. But Moro fought them, saying that she could not marry Pilipili because he was not a Christian. She told them that she had become a Christian and her God refused her to marry one who did not believe in Him. Again she broke loose from the men and ran wildly in the grass. She did not care where she went if only she could hide from them. This she succeeded in doing, for they ran after her but failed to discover her hiding place.

Moro did not know when the men gave up the search, but she was sure that they would be watching all the paths to Ara. She decided that she was less afraid of the wild animals than she was of the men who would take her to Pilipili, so she spent a sleepless night in the tall grass. Her God protected her, and early in the morning she returned to Ara, much relieved that no one was chasing her.

The next time Chief Abok held court, a soldier arrived on

Ara hill demanding that Moro accompany him to the chief's village. Pilipili had brought his case before the chief and Abok called for Moro to explain her side of the affair. The representatives from the various villages, who always attended court to carry home the news of current events, were greatly impressed this day by the unassuming young girl who dared to stand before the chief to declare her faith in God and explain that she could not marry Pilipili because he was not a Christian. They were surprised, however, to hear Chief Abok speak to Pilipili as he did.

"You," he said, "your wife has not refused to go to you. She refuses because you are not a Christian. I am not going to separate you, for you have paid all the wealth on her and she has been with you, but if you want to have her, you must become a Christian too."

Pilipili knew that he must abide by the decision of the paramount chief, so he hastened back to the subchief by whom he was employed and asked to be dismissed from the work of a soldier. As soon as the subchief dismissed him, he went to Ara and presented himself to the missionary, stating that he wanted to become a Christian. His training as a soldier proved profitable, for after being on Ara for two months and giving satisfaction as a new believer, he was made overseer of the girls and boys in their garden work. He went to school with the other workmen, but he was too old to learn easily and never became a fluent reader.

Pilipili did not seek to culminate his marriage with Moro immediately. She continued to go to school and to grow in her knowledge of the path of God. The young Christians at Ara were becoming brave in their witnessing in the villages now. Some of them went out every day. Ukumu, the son of Chief Abok, often walked long distances with a little boy, who went along to carry a drum with which to call the people together so that he could preach to them. It was a great day for Moro when she was allowed to accompany the missionary to the villages. Sometimes the missionary would let her read verses to the people from the Book of God, or quote them from memory.

Each Friday all who had been doing village work met together in a Bible class. In this class, the leader would ask various ones to read a portion from the Book of God, and then the person who read would explain what the verses meant to him. There were other girls who attended, but Moro was the only one who read and entered into the spirit of the class with real earnestness. Even Ukumu and the other boys had to admit that this girl was able to do as well as they, for already she was consumed with a passion for the Book of God which was to characterize her all the rest of her life.

Moro was the first Alur girl to become a teacher of the Word of God in the villages. She could not have been on Ara more than a year when she was assigned to visit certain villages on the plain. A little girl by the name of Pacuwegi, who had attended the mission school for a short time and then gone back to her home at the foot of Ara, went along to carry books and a small folding chair. When Moro went out to teach, she would stop for Pacuwegi and they would hide in the tall grass to pray together before they went any farther. Only then would Moro sit on the chair. When they reached the villages she never used it. Instead she would give it to an old man to sit on. The missionary wanted her to wear shoes to protect her feet while she did so much walking, but she would not do so lest the people in the villages would think her proud and refuse to listen to her message. She was too humble to be seen wearing shoes or sitting on a chair when she went into a village to teach.

Often Moro would have Pacuwegi read the Book of God to the people, whom they had called together under a big tree. Then those who were standing far away in the village would say,

"Look, a little girl is reading the Book. Let us go near and hear her read."

Thus they would gather a crowd and Moro would teach them. At first some of the people made fun of her because she was only a girl. But soon they began to praise her, for she kept her place as a woman while she lovingly shared with them the message of God's salvation. Many, many people came to believe in Moro's Saviour as a result of these village trips. Little Pacuwegi also became brave in confessing Jesus before the people because of the example of Moro. For nearly a year she went with Moro, and the two became lifelong friends.

One day when Moro and Pacuwegi were walking in the villages, they saw a little boy quarreling with his mother and throwing rocks at her.

"Come, let us go to him," said Moro, for this was their third visit to the village and God had given her a great concern for this little boy.

"You had better not go," warned one of the villagers. "He will throw rocks at you."

Moro walked toward little Uminji anyway. When he saw her, he threw on the ground the four rocks which he had in his hand.

"Why are you doing that?" asked Moro gently.

Little Uminji knew by the tone of her voice that she loved him, and he was willing to listen when she told the people of his village about the God who loved them.

"That little fellow! If only he would turn his liver to Jesus, some day you might marry him," Moro said jokingly to Pacuwegi as they left the village that day, not realizing that she was making a prophecy that would come true.

While others on the plain were turning from their time-honored beliefs, Moro's own home village was not left untouched. It was during an epidemic of smallpox which was raging throughout the country that the missionary *bwana* found Moro's half brother, Mugasa, seriously ill. He took him to Ara, where he had the believers build a special hut apart from the others. There Mugasa was given tender care and made a wonderful recovery, though his face still carries scars of the disease. When he saw what the true God had done for him, he left the worship of Jok to serve Him. Soon he had an opportunity to show his gratitude to God, as well as to prove the reality of his faith. Many people around him were dying of sleeping sickness. Most people were afraid to go near them or to touch their bodies, but Mugasa took them food and water, and even buried some of them.

Gem also began to be affected by the continual testimony which he heard from Moro, the missionaries, and other young Christians. One day he burned all his fetishes and all his wives' fetishes, saying that Jok was finishing all his goats for nothing. He was not helping him at all. He also gave up the worship of his deceased father, Bondo, for he knew now that only God could help him.

Akelo, however, resisted all of Moro's pleading. She was still a worshiper of Jok in her heart even though her husband had burned her fetishes. Great was Gem's sorrow when men from a neighboring village came to him to accuse her of being a witch. They said that many of their wives were dying because Akelo was putting sickness into them. But Gem defended Akelo. Because he had become a believer in Jesus, he would not treat her as custom required him to treat a witch. Even though there was interclan war over it, Gem stood firm in his conviction that his wife was not a *jajok.*

Gem was getting old now, and it was not long before he died. But he did not fear death as did the worshipers of Jok around him. Before he went to the Christians' home in Heaven, he exorted his son Mugasa to follow faithfully the path of Jesus about which the missionaries were telling him. So Gem died in the faith, and the missionary gave Mugasa a cloth in which to bury his old father. How thankful Moro was that she would see her father again and that she would not have to appease and worship his departed spirit as he had worshiped Bondo's! It was good that she and her father and her brother Mugasa all walked in the path of the true God.

Chapter 9

A CHRISTIAN WIFE AND MOTHER

WHILE MORO WAS ACTIVE in the village work, studying in the mission school, and carrying on her duties in the *madamo's* kitchen, Pilipili gave every evidence of having left the paths of darkness and seemed to be making progress as a Christian. He was not known to take part in any practices connected with the worship of Jok. He no longer drank beer. He did not go to the sensuous heathen dances. He attended regularly the services in the little mission chapel. He was enrolled in the class of those who were being prepared for baptism. He was dependable in his work as overseer of the gardens. So when he began to build a new hut on Ara hill, Moro knew that she could not refuse him any longer.

At a simple Christian ceremony, performed by the missionary *bwana,* Moro and Pilipili were pronounced man and wife, and they began their life together in the new hut. Moro realized now that she never could leave him, for they had been united in the name of the true God whom they both professed to know and love.

The young bride entered wholeheartedly into her new duties as a housewife. There were waterpots which she must keep filled. She must weed the gardens which Pilipili had started for them. She spent many of her first days of married life in the tall grass gathering wood and storing it in their hut. This was not to be used except in emergencies. Each week she made as many trips as necessary to gather wood for current needs. Daily the grain must be ground into flour for the big meal. On her knees, bending over the big grinding stone, she would rub a smaller stone rhythmically back and forth over it, crushing the grain as she did so. The village women always sang sad chants as they did this, but Moro loved to sing Gospel songs.

There was not much time in this busy life for her to attend school, but she never missed the Bible classes. Nor did her husband require her to give up her village work. It was a great delight to Moro to be able to continue her walks in the villages. Many women came to Ara to hear the words of God because of Moro's constant invitations, and some of them believed on Him. Pilipili had planted a garden of potatoes in his home village, so Moro had to make frequent trips to Awasi, about two hours' walk from Ara, to get potatoes for their meals. Balancing a big basket on her head, she would take the precious Book of God in her hand, and she found many opportunities to tell about her Saviour as she went back and forth between Awasi and Ara.

On these trips, Moro discovered that some of the boys who had studied in class with her had gone as far as Awasi giving out the words of God, but they had not had a warm reception there. The people of the village were completely given over to the worship of Jok and the appeasing of the spirits of the dead. Moro was sad about this, and she prayed much for the people of her husband's home village, for not one of them had turned to the true God.

As the industrious young wife went cheerfully about the task of making a Christian home, it was not long before she became happy in the anticipation of motherhood. However, her joy soon turned to sorrow. Before the appointed time she had given birth to a tiny baby boy, but he never breathed a breath in this world. Now a small mound of earth marked the place where the little one was buried, and Moro learned the new lesson that the heavenly Father was the God of all comfort.

On September 17, 1922, when Moro was about twenty years old, seventeen believers from Kasengu and twenty from Ara met at the river Ttada to make public confession of their faith through baptism. The heathen passed around rumors that those who dared to have sin hidden in their hearts when they went under the water would drown. Moro, who was one of the number from Ara that day, could not be frightened by such rumors, for she knew that her sins had been washed away by the blood of Jesus.

Because many African names were those of evil spirits or names of sadness, it was the custom for believers to take a name from the Bible upon receiving baptism. Moro had been greatly impressed by the life of Phebe, who was "a servant of the church" and "a succorer of many," including the men who were preaching the Gospel. She wanted her life to be a blessing in the church even as the life of this godly woman had been, so she chose the name of Phebe, which had been translated into her language as Sheeba.

Two years after her baptism, the Lord saw fit to answer Moro Sheeba's prayer for a child, and she gave birth to a baby boy who was perfect in every way. She named the baby after the prophet Daniel, who had purposed in his heart to serve the only true God, praying that her little Daniel might grow up to love and serve Him just as faithfully. Daniel was a healthy little boy and a great delight to his mother. He loved to have her sing him to sleep as she rocked him back and forth on her back, and when he began to walk and to say a few words, she taught him the name of Jesus. Soon he learend to point up to Heaven when his mother would ask him where Jesus was, and to open his little arms to everybody when she asked him whom Jesus loved.

Sometimes Moro Sheeba would tie little Daniel on her back,

put a woven-basket hood over his head to protect him from sun or rain, and go to her home village to visit her old mother. Great was her consternation one day when she found that Akelo was not there. Since Gem had died, there was no one to defend her and she had been chased away as a witch. Later, when Sheeba heard that her mother had ventured back to her village again, after trying in vain to find a place to stay among some people of the Kebu tribe, she brought her to Ara.

At Ara the Christians built a small hut for Akelo near the hut of her daughter. At last she had a place to live and need not roam the country any more. She was deeply touched by the love of the Christians on Ara when they allowed her to live among them. Moro taught her mother faithfully until finally Akelo believed on the Son of God. Everyone knew that she had believed, for her life was changed. Joy was in her heart and on her face, and she delighted to attend the services on the mission station.

By this time missionaries had been living on Ara for more than ten years, and a thriving church had been established there. Moro had watched it grow almost from the beginning when she and Ukumu and others of the early believers had spelled out their first words in the thatched chapel-school. The chief's son, now known as Yohana Ukumu, was no longer at Ara. He had been called by the government officials back to his father's village to help in the work of the kingdom. The wisdom of numbers which he had learned in the mission school had made it possible for him to be put in charge of the taxes. What his classmates did not know, however, was that the Belgians wanted him under observation, because his father had expressed a desire that this son rule in his place when he died, and that some day Mukamboland would be ruled by a Christian chief.

Little Pacuwegi, who had gone with Moro when she began to teach in the villages, was growing up now. Her fellow girls had given her the "praise" name of Usiga and when she was baptized she took the Christian name of Hana. Uminji, the little fellow whom she and Moro had found throwing rocks at his mother, had come to Ara also, and had grown into a young man who dearly loved the Jesus about whom they had been the first to tell him. He too was baptized and went by the name of Solimon. Moro Sheeba was delighted when she learned that Solimon Uminji's father was paying wealth on Hana Usiga. So her joking prediction was going to be fulfilled! Their romance was very different from that of Moro's for they truly loved one another, and her joy was great when she saw them united in Christian marriage.

Moro Sheeba would have been glad to have lived always in the happy Christian community at Ara, but Pilipili was not of the same mind. For a long time he had been determined to move back to his family village, Awasi. Sometimes he insisted so strongly that it was all his wife could do to dissuade him. The matter came to a crisis, however, in the month of March when Daniel was a little more than a year and a half old. It was the month of digging the ground to plant millet. Pilipili announced one day that he had given up his work as headman over the boys' and girls' gardens at Ara, and informed Moro Sheeba that they were going to Amasi to dig their millet garden and gather materials for a hut.

Sheeba knew it was useless to object further, though she took care to make provision for one important problem that was facing her. Very soon she was to have another little one, and she did not want to give birth to her child in the heathen village because of the many evil customs which she would be urged to follow. Therefore she made arrangements for her mother to care for Daniel on Ara, while she would go back and forth to Awasi to help her husband.

The government was discouraging the people from building the old-style huts with grass all the way to the ground, because such huts were a haven for rats and fleas that carried the dreaded bubonic plague. So Pilipili built his hut with mud walls like those on the mission station. The men of the village helped him to gather the poles and elephant grass that were needed for the framework. It fell to Moro's lot to pull many, many loads of tall grass for the roof, which she did with some assistance from the wives of some of Pilipili's village brothers.

When the elephant grass had been tied to the outside of the circular framework, the villagers held a mudding bee, throwing handfuls of mud at the elephant grass wall to force it between the cracks of the grass until it was entirely covered with mud both inside and outside. After this had dried for several days, Moro had to go over it again with a thinner mixture of mud and then "varnish" it with cow manure. The floor was made of anthill dirt, pounded fine, spread evenly on the ground, dampened, and beaten until it was hard. When this was dry and received its coats of "varnish," Moro made neat fireplaces of rocks for cooking her food and a clay circle on the floor to support her earthen pots. In the meantime the men had tied the grass on the roof and the hut was ready for occupancy.

Moro Sheeba had to help her husband dig his garden, for as Christians they would not have beer drinks in order to get others to come and dig for them. Their old gardens had to be looked after too, but Moro was glad for an excuse to make frequent trips to the mission station. She was especially glad that, when the hut at Awasi was finished, the corn and peanuts, beans, and semsem which they had planted on Ara were ready to harvest, for she could be working there right up to the time when her baby was due. So that was where Daniel's baby brother, Matayo, put in his appearance one sunny afternoon in June. But the harvesting of the crops and the birth of Matayo meant also that Moro's happy life at Ara had come to an end. Now she must face what it was actually to live at Awasi.

Chapter 10

A SHEEP AMONG WOLVES

NOW THAT IT WAS no longer possible for Moro Sheeba to live among the Christians on Ara, she was desirous that her move to Awasi should be a demonstration of the power of God over the evil spirits whom her people worshiped. To travel with a newborn infant was absolutely forbidden by the heathen, for they lived in terror of Adranga, the spirit in the streams, and of the spirits in the rocks and mountains, all of whom took a peculiar delight in causing sickness in the newborn. Therefore, as soon as she was allowed to come out of the hut, three days after baby Matayo was born and even before he had turned black,[1] Moro determined to make the journey with him to her husband's village.

Knowing full well how her action would be regarded, Moro stooped over and put Matayo on her back, holding his little hand under her chin while she adjusted the hood over his head and place the animal-skin carrier around him. Then, grasping the straps which were attached to the four corners of the carrier, she straightened up and twisted them together on her chest. With Matayo thus secured on her back, she turned deliberately to take the path which led down the hill Ara and over the plain past the villages where she was known and where

[1]African babies are very light in color when they are born. It is only after from one to several weeks that their skin becomes black.

her people lived. She knew that God had given her this baby boy and that He would protect him. The simple love and trust in the true God left no place in her heart to fear and appease the evil spirits who were deceiving her loved ones.

Not far from the foot of Ara was the stream Wali. With a "cool liver," Moro crossed this stream, walked past the big rocks that were by the wayside, and looked toward the mountains on her left, thanking God that she knew now that He was the Creator of these things and that hence they were in His power.

"*Aka! Aka! Aka!*" shrieked the old women on the plain, throwing up their arms and shaking their heads in terror.

"Oh, Moro, Moro, what are you doing? Have you gone crazy? You're killing your child," they shouted at her.

These were Moro Sheeba's village relatives. They had seen her cross the stream and pass the rocks and mountains—and the foolhardy girl had not even taken the precaution to throw grain and red clay to the spirits as she did so.

"Surely the evil spirits will be displeased and kill the child," they said to one another.

With their scanty covering of leaves and their *uposhos* hanging down behind, they stood before Moro with pleading eyes. The crystal sticks in their lower lips bobbed up and down as they talked to her, and the charms on their arms waved with their excited gestures. They wondered what this child of theirs would have to say in defense of her reckless behavior. Did she not know that her milk would dry up and her baby would die?

"God, who created my baby, will protect him," Moro told them with confidence. "It is He who created the streams and the rocks and the mountains. I worship Him and the things which He created."

Leaving this testimony with them, Moro continued on her way. The old women sat sorrowfully with their heads bowed over their knees, their *uposhos* drawn up between their legs and thrown over one hip. They had warned her, but she had refused to listen to them. Now they would await the news from Awasi that would tell them of the baby's death.

The misunderstanding which she had encountered by the way was to be Moro Sheeba's daily portion at Awasi. At first the women welcomed her when she came with her children to live among them, for they anticipated her partnership in all of their affairs. But when they discovered that she would have nothing to do with their heathen customs, they began to take offense and leave her alone.

Thus Moro was cast more completely upon the Lord. Not only did she find that He could sustain her through this trial, but she learned consistently to show kindness toward those who were unkind to her, although it was not always easy to do so. Nor did she stop telling everyone she could about the only true God.

Sheeba did not fear to witness to the old and important people of the village, even though custom decreed that a young wife should not speak to these older men. She was particularly concerned for Ajika, the subchief who ruled under Chief Abok over the several hundred interrelated people of Awasi and its satellite villages. Ajika was getting very old and feeble at the time when Moro came to live in her husband's village. Pilipili called him his father, for he was the brother of Pilipili's father who had died.

"Father-in-law," she would say to Ajika, "I want you to believe in Jesus."

Others who were present said Sheeba did badly because she was teaching him about Jesus, and they wanted him to give a goat so they could sacrifice.

"You are a fool," they told Moro Sheeba.

But old Ajika did not scorn the words of his brother's daughter-in-law as others did, and she had reason to think that he believed. Ajika did not live long after Moro talked to him about

Jesus. When he died she took her Book and stood by his grave where the death dance was going on. There she told the people all that she found in the words of God about death.

"*Eh-h-h!* Do women teach the words of God?" mocked some.

"In the strength of God, I do teach His Word," she answered them.

Even though the villagers made fun of her and did all they could to stop her, whenever anyone died she went to the graveside with the Book of God and taught the people there.

Ajika's tall slender son, Upio, who had been helping him to rule for some time, became the new subchief. Upio p'Ajika was unimpressed by what Sheeba had taught his father and gave himself wholly to serving Jok and the spirits of the dead. He lost no time in calling together the witch doctors and the elders of the village for the big ceremony of placing the seven *abila* sticks in the ground in front of his hut door so that Ajika's spirit could rest upon them and watch over his household. Constantly he led the people of Awasi in the worship of the spirits of Ajika and other departed members of the clan.

As Moro continued to witness and live for the Lord in this place, refusing to sacrifice on any occasion, she was the object of persistent abuse. Sometimes people awakened to find that for spite someone had left an evil omen by their door. They were very frightened when this happened because they believed that a spirit had left the omen to show his displeasure with the occupant of the hut. One night Moro happened to see Pilipili's brother come to her door in the dark and leave this omen. In the morning, when the village people saw it, they were greatly stirred.

"You are spoiling everything," they told her. "We never eat sacrificed meat any more because of your teaching of the words of God. Jok is displeased with you and has shown you so by this. Stop teaching the words of God."

"No, I must give out the words of God. I am not afraid," she replied. "It was Pilipili's brother. I saw him."

To Pilipili she said, "Is that the custom of you and the people in your village? Go and take away the evil omen."

Several times this evil act was done at Moro's door. An old woman at Awasi, who had been chased from her husband's village as a *jajok,* treated her that way twice. Each time the women were greatly disturbed and pleaded with Moro to give up teaching the words of God lest she die. But Moro was not to be moved. They were astonished that she was not afraid of Jok as they were, and gradually her fearless attitude began to make an impression upon them.

When Moro's own relatives heard what the old *jajok* did, they were incensed and went to her half brother Mugasa, saying,

"Why do you not go to Awasi and make war with those people for treating your sister that way?"

When Moro heard this, she went to Mugasa and begged him not to go.

"I have forgiven them for all they have done to me," she told him. "Do not scold them. I take my stand in God's name, in Jesus' name."

Mugasa, being one with her in her faith, never caused trouble over the matter. So intense was Moro Sheeba's desire to win the people of Awasi to believe in Jesus, that she maintained this same loving attitude toward all who hated her, and she went out of her way to do kind things for everyone in the village. When someone was ill, she always went to help that person. When the big chief Abok would come to visit Upio p'Ajika, she would cook delicious food and take it to the subchief to welcome his guest. In time both men and women were forced to respect the kind, courageous young wife of Pilipili. While some still stayed away from her and others made fun of her, there were those who began to be glad when they had an opportunity to hear more about the God of love who had made her so different from the rest of them.

Chapter 11

THE AFFAIR OF MAKING BEER

SOON AFTER THE MOVE to Awasi, Pilipili had begun to show his true colors, and Moro was grieved to find that his faith in the true God was only a sham. To him it had been but a necessary form in order to take possession of the wife for whom he had paid his wealth. Now that he had her here with his heathen relatives at last, there was no need to keep up the pretense that had been so successful at Ara. As nephew to the subchief, he was a person of importance in Awasi, and he made up his mind that his wife would have to obey him. They must have big gardens in keeping with their station, and the only way to get them was by having a beer drink.

"Take this grain and put it to soak in the stream," he ordered Moro one day.

She knew that soaking grain in the stream could be for only one purpose and questioned him. He stormed at her, reminding her that she was his property and that she should do as he said without any questions.

"I am willing to obey you," she told him, "for you are my husband, but if you tell me to do something that my God tells me not to do, then I will have to refuse. Are you not also a believer in the true God? Why do you demand that I make beer?"

"There is no other way to have big gardens dug," insisted Pilipili.

When Moro refused to make beer for her husband, the old men of the village continually kept at him to assert his authority over her.

"Compel your wife to make beer," they urged him. "If your wife does not make beer, your village will not abide well."

"A woman! Only a woman!" they snorted contemptuously. "Of course she will make beer. You are a great person, Pilipili. She *will* make beer."

Day after day and month after month the threats continued. Pilipili, the subchief Upio p'Ajika, the village elders, and even her fellow women were relentless in their demands that Moro Sheeba make beer for her husband so that he might have big gardens. She offered to kill and cook chickens enough to feed the diggers. But did they want chickens? No, they wanted beer! Life became so unbearable with the constant nagging and threatening that finally Moro began to wonder if it might not be best, after all, to give in and do as her husband said. She would not have to drink the beer. After holding out for a year, she yielded to the demands that were being made of her, but only her God knew the agony in the heart of His child as she made and served beer for the digging of a garden. On two occasions when Pilipili wanted gardens dug, Sheeba made and served the beer to the men who dug them. Pilipili and his heathen village brothers rejoiced over their victory. At last they had succeeded in bringing this woman into subjection to them.

Moro Sheeba was distressed at having to bring up her two little boys in an atmosphere such as this, with beer being made in their own home and degrading customs being practiced all around them. Because of this she determined to teach them to read while they were very young so that they might know the Book of God for themselves and be influenced to take the path of Jesus. Little Daniel was only about three years of age when she pulled out the flash cards that had been given to her by the missionaries and used them to teach him "a—e—i—o—u" and the consonants to go with the vowels. Then she would write short words on the mud wall of their hut with the white sap from a fresh banana stalk. At the same time, she taught Daniel to write on the ground with his finger.

The first book from which his mother taught Daniel to read was what the people called *Yohana ma Tar,* the White John. The White John was the First Epistle of John, so called because of its white cover and thus distinguished from the Black John, which was John's Gospel with the black cover—for at that time, as fast as the books of the Bible were translated into Moro Sheeba's language, they were printed one by one in separate books.

As little Daniel learned to read the White John, his mother began to teach him from this book: "Every man that hath this hope in him purifieth himself, even as he is pure." It was a favorite verse of Sheeba's. From this verse she taught her little boy that he could not be disobedient and still be a pure child of God. Thus he learned that disobedience and many other things were wrong, because they were not pure. The grown-up Daniel admits having been lazy and having had a far greater desire to play with the other children, but he recalls how his mother would get him and bring him into their hut for his lessons. Indeed, it was not long before the other village children were gathered in by Moro Sheeba and taught both how to read and about the God of her Book.

When Daniel was about five and had learned to read very well, Sheeba heard the men talking together about another garden that must be dug. That meant that she would be compelled a third time to make beer for her husband and his village brothers and friends. But as she read in her White John, the God in whom she had believed convicted her of trying to serve two masters. It was the same verse which she had been teaching

Daniel that spoke to her: "Every man that hath this hope in him purifieth himself, even as he is pure."

God seemed to be saying to her, "How can you take My Word in your hands and teach Daniel and his playmates to be pure, when you use those same hands to make and serve beer which causes people to do and say impure things?"

Moro's heart was torn and a mighty conflict raged within. How could she defy the demands of her owner? What could she, one lone Christian in a heathen village—and only a woman—do? But in all the conflict there was one certainty. She knew that Jesus was her Saviour. She believed in Him. She loved Him and wanted to serve Him. Then her decision was made. She must be the right example to her children at any cost. She would be true to God even unto death. She would not make beer even if it cost her life. Once the decision was made, it was not difficult for Moro Sheeba to refuse, for God was with her and she found His grace sufficient.

"What! Not make beer any more! Are you crazy?" exploded Pilipili. "You *must* make beer!"

But Sheeba calmly replied, "I read in the Book of God that it is wrong. Even though you kill me, I cannot do it again."

This uncompromising ultimatum ushered in a period of relentless persecution over the affair of beer. Moro's meek and quiet spirit quivered under the harsh treatment of her husband. He dragged her before the village elders as they sat around the fire of the *kadipo* at night. There the subchief Upio threatened to whip her if she did not submit, only to be told,

"You may whip me if you wish, but I cannot make beer."

Time and again Moro was dragged before the elders at the *kadipo* or she was beaten by her husband, but always with the same result. Thus thwarted, Pilipili had to resort to other means to get his gardens dug. He would give a goat to the diggers and let them use it to buy their own beer. Or he would call in other village women to make the beer in his hut. Sometimes the women who were cooking the beer would step outside for a few minutes and Moro, going into her hut to get something, would find the beer boiling over. Ordinarily she would have rushed to the aid of her fellow women, but now she must stand firm, so she would pay no attention to the beer, much to the disgust of the women when they would re-enter and find the fire out.

It was not long before Pilipili began to feel sorry for himself and even to refuse to drink beer with the other men. He would help his fellow villagers dig their gardens but deny himself the privilege of drinking with them when the work was done. How could he drink the beer of others when he could not reciprocate in proper fashion? It was a very humiliating position for the head of a household and an important man in the village of Upio p'Ajika.

While all this was going on, Moro Sheeba, confident that God would honor one who honored Him, decided to do something that would prove this to the village people. She would plant food before the mixing of the seeds and the blessing of Won Angu, an elaborate heathen ceremony performed in the fields by an elder who had power to commune with the spirits of the dead. It was the firm belief of every heathen Alur that his seed would not otherwise grow or bear harvest. To get ahead of the blessing of Won Angu, she would have to dig before the rains came while the ground was still dry and hard. Her husband would have waited for the rites, and the people would have stopped her had they known her intention, so Moro did not dare to let anyone know when she slipped out of the village, hoe in hand, and with her own hands dug small gardens and planted them. It was too late to protest when the sprouted gardens were discovered, and no doubt it furnished food for thought for the villagers when they saw these little gardens bear a greater harvest than the gardens of all the others.

The gardens made an impression on little Daniel as well,

for he could not help but notice that the big gardens which his father had dug for the price of beer did not bear as well as those of his mother, small though they were. His parents were praying to different gods, and truly his mother's God seemed to be more powerful.

Neither did the fact go unobserved by the village folk that, save in the matter of making beer, Moro was a faithful wife. Her hut was always clean and in repair. The sliding door of split bamboo that closed it up at night was kept "varnished" with fresh cow dung so that there were no pieces of old dung flaking off to leave messy holes. There was always an adequate supply of firewood on hand, and water for bathing and cooking. She cooked savory meals and served them with all the deference due her husband. She tried to plant in her gardens the things that would please him, for she did not wish to make him angry. Her children were well and lovingly cared for. She did not shirk her own work, nor did she fail to lend a helping hand to others who needed her ministrations.

At last Pilipili's brother, Musasi, realizing what a faithful wife Moro Sheeba was to him, began to suggest to Pilipili that he cease trying to compel her to make beer. But Pilipili stubbornly refused to heed such nonsense. Finally, in great anger, he brought Moro Sheeba before the village court where Upio p'Ajika presided and was assisted by all the important elders of the village.

After they had reprimanded Sheeba for not making beer, they allowed her to speak. Once again she tried to explain to them why she was refusing. It was because God's Book taught her it was wrong. Then, opening her little Book, the *Yohana ma Tar,* she read I John 3:3 to them and said,

"This verse teaches me that I must be clean, be holy, even as the true God is holy, and I can't obey Him if I make beer."

"She is a good woman," said Upio p'Ajika when Moro had spoken. "She is a good housekeeper and she cooks for you well.

But something in this Book of hers keeps her from making beer. Why don't you let her alone?"

The village elders were of the same opinion as Upio now. This was too much for Pilipili. It infuriated him. Even his own relatives were taking his wife's part. He would show them that he was the head of his house. Breathlessly the women, who had gathered around the outer circle of the court to hear Sheeba's fate, listened to Pilipili's answer,

"She is *only* a woman. She is *my* property. She *cannot* refuse my words. If she does not make beer, I'll kill her."

"You have heard what Pilipili has said," Upio commented, turning to Sheeba. "Are you going to make beer, or what are you going to do?"

With a holy boldness Moro answered, "I will do all his work well, but though he kill me I cannot make beer."

Fear was written on the countenance of every woman. Not one among them would have dared to stand against the threats of the man who had bought them for sheep and goats. As it started to get dark that night, some of Moro's village sisters, who had been bought by Pilipili's village brothers, came to her and pleaded with her to take refuge with them.

"Pilipili is very angry," they said. "He will kill you tonight if you stay in his hut. Come, come and sleep with one of us."

"I am doing this for the true God," Moro told her village sisters. "I am looking to Him to take care of me. I am going to sleep in my own hut."

So she left them and went into the hut, spread her mat on the floor, and lay down. After a time, she heard the gathering at the *kadipo* break up and the men going to their respective huts. What would Pilipili do now? She lay very still and prayed as she heard him enter and slide the split-bamboo door in place.

Pilipili walked straight to the center of the hut to the shelf on the bamboo poles. He took down his mat, unrolled it, and lay down without making so much as a move toward his wife—

and that was the last day that he ever mentioned anything to her about making beer. Moro took courage from this and broke all the beer pots that belonged to her. Some of them were in the hut of her mother-in-law. These also she fetched and broke.

After this the village elders took their "livers" off of Moro Sheeba. That is, they gave it up as a hopeless case trying to get her to make beer. Even Pilipili began to realize that drinking beer was really bad, for it made him do terrible things. It was after a beer drink, in which they had had too much to drink, that he had quarreled with Upio and started toward him in great anger with his spear and bow and arrows, and might have done him much harm had not Upio and another man snatched his weapons and broken them to pieces. Although he would not yet admit it, even then the God of Moro Sheeba was reminding Pilipili that his wife was right in trying to hinder him from drinking beer.

Chapter 12

A FAMILY UNITED

"SHEEBA, how can one believe in Jesus?"

The question came from five-year-old Daniel one day shortly after his mother had ceased to make beer for his father. What joy was in Moro Sheeba's heart as she dropped what she was doing and picked up the Black John! Opening it, she read to him from the third chapter:

"He that believeth on the Son hath everlasting life: and he that believeth not the Son shall not see life; but the wrath of God abideth on him."

Patiently and thoroughly Sheeba explained exactly what it meant to believe on the Son of God, for the intelligent questions which Daniel went on asking assured her that her child was not far from the kingdom of God. With her heart uplifted in silent prayer, she continued to answer him until he understood clearly and declared his faith in Jesus Christ. Then she read Romans 10:9, 10 from a little booklet which she had, teaching him what the words meant.

"Now," she finished, "you must confess Jesus before others. You may confess him in our class which I am teaching."

By this time there were some among Moro Sheeba's village neighbors who were ready to listen to what she had to tell about the true God, and they were meeting frequently for her to teach them from her Book. That day when she had gathered her little Bible class together, she gave Daniel an opportunity to tell what he had done.

"*Tin ayio Yesu* (Today I have accepted Jesus)," said the little fellow simply, and then, as he tells the story now, his heart was filled with much joy as one who has discovered great wealth.

Young as he was, his mother realized before many months that Daniel had made a definite transaction with God. Unquestionably he had experienced the new birth. Neither was there any hesitation on the part of the church elders in permitting him to receive baptism two years later, when he was seven, so well had he been grounded in the Word of God.

Even when he was five, Daniel began to be a help to his mother with Matayo and the other village children who had gathered around and begged to be taught with her two boys. Many times she would leave him teaching the class while she went to see about her cooking, for she never neglected her household duties in spite of the responsibility of teaching this growing class of children. But the class became a new grounds for persecution at the hands of the subchief, the village elders, and even her husband.

"You, a woman!" they would sneer. "Teaching children in school! Are you equal to such a work?"

Then they would order the children to be taken out of school, and they treated them as prisoners. Some of them were sent to the big chief to work for him as punishment for having gone.

"Children, do not be afraid," Moro would say to them quietly when they returned from their punishment. "Come on to school. Come back to school."

And the children would come. Again and again Upio p'Ajika and the elders tried to put an end to her school until finally Sheeba appealed to the missionaries on Ara for help. When they had called the subchief and reasoned with him, he stopped persecuting her openly for her work of teaching. The missionaries also encouraged her by giving her a young fellow by the name of Yakobo to help her. But Upio resorted to another strategy to keep her from teaching the village children. He would keep her so busy that she would have no time to teach. Accordingly he and the village elders continually gave her the task of preparing food for the paramount chief or for the porters of the government officials when they visited the village.

Moro shouldered the new burdens with a cheerful spirit, but they did not keep her from teaching the children. Not only so, but she went about from hut to hut and from garden to garden, telling the people about how they might have everlasting life. Daniel would go along with her to carry her books and sometimes she would allow him to help her do God's work by reading for her. In fact, so eager was she to have her little boy doing the work of God that she sent him to carry the drum for young Yakobo when he went every morning to the more distant villages which had no one to teach them the Gospel. Yakobo and Daniel would return to Awasi with many people from these villages who wanted to learn how to read and write, so they would attend the school which Sheeba and Yakobo were teaching in the afternoon—and it grew.

In the midst of this busy life, Moro Sheeba was called upon to spend anxious days over the illness of her younger child. Even though he was very sick, she firmly refused to sacrifice for him and gave thanks to the true God when he began to get better. Then she noticed a swelling just below Matayo's ear, a swelling which increased at an alarming rate. Now Upio p'Ajika came daily to insist that a sacrifice be made to the spirit of the dead. When Moro saw that the people of the village were determined to sacrifice, she could endure it no longer, so she called a friend to help her with the children and the load of food and started out on the long journey to Rethy where there was a missionary doctor. Their first stop was at Ara. Sheeba's calmness and faith were a blessing to everyone there, but even the missionaries wondered if the little one would live to reach Rethy.

Matayo was still alive when they got to their journey's end and his mother was encouraged to notice a slight decrease in the swelling. As she turned him over to the missionary doctor and his wife, she informed them that the glory of the true God was at stake and she knew that He had power to heal her child. For two months they ministered tenderly to the little boy until he was well. During that time, Upio p'Ajika sent Pilipili's brother with a few of the village girls to carry food to Moro and the children and to inquire as to the welfare of the sick one. So amazed was he at their report when they returned that he himself made the long journey to see his cousin's child. When Matayo was brought home well, many at Awasi began to listen more often to what Moro Sheeba was teaching, wondering what evil spirit or spirit of the dead could help them as Moro's God had helped her.

As her little boys grew older, Moro Sheeba exercised great care over their training. Frequently she would sit down to have heart-to-heart talks with them, telling them often the story of Hannah and Samuel and of how she had given them to God to do His work, even as Hannah had given Samuel. She never allowed them to play with the other village children unless she was near them, lest they learn to curse and do evil things. Nor would she leave them in the village when she went on a visit elsewhere. Even when she went as far as Ara, she would take them.

The year 1929, which marked the end of the strife over the affair of beer, was also a year of other severe trials that proved the power of Moro's faith in the eyes of the heathen village people. It was during this year that she gave birth to baby Yohana, but before he had turned black, God took the little one back to Himself. Moro leaned once more on her God for comfort and rejoiced that her family was gathering up in Heaven, for Akelo had slipped away to be with Jesus soon after her daughter's move to Awasi.

In December of the year that baby Yohana died, Pilipili was stricken with a serious infection. So swollen were his foot and leg that the relatives swarmed around him with grave concern.

"Truly we must appease the spirits lest our brother die," wailed his village brothers.

But Moro Sheeba would not permit any sacrificing. Kindly but firmly she stood her ground against them.

"You may not sacrifice to the evil spirits for Pilipili's swollen leg," she said. "They have no power to heal him. Come, fix a carrying chair and carry him up the big escarpment to the missionary doctor. The doctor is a servant of the true God who has power to heal."

"You're a fool," they told her. "And who will dig gardens for you if you let your husband die? We must *twi ayitha. Twi ayitha* anyway, or his leg will be stiff and he will never walk again even if he does get better."

Pilipili's village brothers were quite ready to give of their wealth to *twi ayitha.* They would give a goat to the prophet to tell them that a sacrifice with the medicine of *ayitha* must be made. They would give another one to the witch doctor so that he would come to tie the medicine on Pilipili's swollen leg. They would give a chicken to sacrifice and throw to the mountains and another goat to be sacrificed that its blood and its liver might be rubbed on the *ayitha* stick. While the sacrificial meat was being roasted, the witch doctor would say to the people who were gathered around,

"Go away. The smoke of this fire might bring the same sickness to you."

Then he would make away with the meat for himself, and Pilipili's relatives would have to give him a hoe or arrows for the use of the knife with which he killed th sacrifice. This is the procedure they were determined to follow for the restoration of Pilipili.

Moro Sheeba tried to tell her husband's relatives how Jok was deceiving them and would finish all their wealth. As she persisted in her refusal to permit them to sacrifice, finally they agreed to carry Pilipili as far as Sheeba's home village. From there she could get her own relatives to help her get him to a doctor. With the aid of her Christian brother, Mugasa, and other men who were believers, they accomplished the remainder of the long and difficult journey to Rethy, over the path so recently taken by Moro when little Matayo was ill.

"Had you delayed one day longer," the doctor told them when he had seen the patient, "Pilipili would have died."

God had heard Moro Sheeba's prayers and made a way before it was too late. Now much prayer was made to the true God to heal Pilipili's leg for His own glory, that the heathen might see His power and that He hears the prayers of those who follow Him. For three months they stayed at Rethy while Pilipili received treatment and regained his strength. By then he could walk again—just as he used to walk. The news had traveled back to Awasi, so everyone was out to see him walk into his own village on his own two feet.

What was Pilipili saying?

"If it had not been for the faith of my wife, you would have sacrificed for me and I would have died. I never want to have anything to do with heathen sacrifices again, for it was the true God who spared my life and allowed me to walk again."

The heathen relatives were speechless, for they knew what Pilipili was saying was true. What was more, he went on to say that no longer would he join them in digging gardens for a drink of beer, and he said it so that everyone knew he meant it. This was not the same Pilipili who had left them three months before. His face was shining now with an inward joy, just like Moro Sheeba's. They could see the outer miracle that had healed his leg, but they failed to comprehend the inner miracle of healing in his soul that had made him of one spirit with his wife.

Chapter 13

INCREASE IN THE HOUSEHOLD OF FAITH

A NEW LIFE BEGAN for Moro Sheeba with the true conversion of Pilipili. In place of discord there was love in the home as husband and wife, together with their children, prayed daily to the true God and sought to serve Him. Nor were they at this time the only believers in Awasi, for a cousin of Pilipili's had gone to Ara, heard the Gospel there, and had become a believer. This cousin, whose name was Filipo, had chosen a wife from among the girls who were Christians, and they had established their home at Awasi.

Sheeba had agreed to act as hostess in place of Filipo's mother when his young bride, Sipora, had come to his village with her fellow girls from her home village, for they did not want to follow the heathen marriage customs. Sipora went to her husband's hut, but the other girls stayed with Moro. When they had fulfilled their week of helping Sipora with her gardens, she saw them safely out of the village and well along the path that led to their home. Throughout her life, whenever there was a marriage, no matter whether the visiting girls were Christians or heathen, she would manage somehow to take them to her hut.

Shortly before Pilipili had been taken to Rethy, a young

married man by the name of Simon Ugwoko had arrived to relieve Moro Sheeba of the school, which had grown surprisingly in spite of the persecution. He shared also in the responsibilities of evangelistic and church services, and now there was a little thatched chapel-school at Awasi. Simon's coming freed Moro to walk more among the people. Her husband was willing for her to go also to the villages of all the surrounding country. She was a familiar figure on the paths, carrying little Matayo, or later his baby sister Rodia, on her back. Continually, in the gardens, under the shade trees, at their fireplaces, in the yard, or on the path she would share the good news of her God with her fellow women.

Occasionally she would go to her home village to visit Mugasa and the other relatives. She was particularly interested in the wife of the headman in a village through which she had to pass on these trips, so she always stopped there for a drink of water and took time to tell this woman about the true God. So impressed was the headman's wife after a number of conversations that she inquired if there was a place nearby where she could go to hear more, and in time she believed in Moro Sheeba's God.

One of the first women at Awasi to turn from serving Jok was Uriemo, a wife of the subchief, Upio. Uriemo carried a certain charm which she must keep through her entire lifetime because of a curse under which she was born. She wore also the *ngisa* charm, even as Akelo had done, to signify that she had been possessed by evil spirits, and she assisted her husband in his witchcraft. But in time she began to be weary of the chains that bound her and longed to be free like Moro Sheeba.

Moro instructed this woman faithfully from the Book of God, telling her that she could not serve both Jok and the true God, that she would have to choose between them, that the *ngisa* and the other charm belonged to the affairs of Jok. She did not urge Uriemo, but she spent hours praying for her and the other village women. It was a glad day when the subchief's wife came to her, saying,

"I want to take Jesus for my Saviour. Here are my witchcraft things and the charms for you to burn."

After Uriemo had become a Christian, Moro Sheeba taught her to read. She could not learn as quickly as the children, but her teacher was patient with her, knowing that she needed to read the Book of God daily, encouraging her to obtain a copy of her own. This Uriemo did, by making and selling earthen pots to earn the price of it. Now Uriemo became Moro's right-hand helper. When the grass on the little chapel-school began to rot, causing the building to leak, it was Uriemo who would go to the bush with Moro to bring in loads of grass to mend the roof. When the mud walls began to crumble and all the other village women refused to help, Uriemo worked with Moro to repair them. At Christmas time, and on other special occasions when meetings would be held on Ara for the building up of the Christians, Moro always took Uriemo with her to share the fellowship.

One day Uriemo had such a severe headache that she was not able to cook for her husband. Upio p'Ajika had been waiting for such an opportunity to upbraid her for burning her witchcraft. Now he exploded and took things in his own hands.

"You have displeased the evil spirit which possessed you," he told her. "We will sacrifice again so that it may be appeased."

Uriemo refused her husband in vain. The witch doctor was called, but before he could get there Moro Sheeba had taken her to her own hut for protection. Upio and village elders surrounded Moro's hut and demanded that she let them have Uriemo. But Sheeba met them fearlessly in spite of their flashing spears and bows and arrows—and they did not get Uriemo.

"If she dies, it will be you who killed her," they warned as they stomped off to their villages, outraged to have been outwitted by a woman.

That was not the only time that Uriemo ran to Sheeba for protection. Once when the locusts had fallen in great swarms, she had gathered many of them and fixed a savory dish to go with the thick mush of the evening meal. After she had served the men, she enjoyed a good serving of the locusts herself. During the night, however, her stomach became very swollen. Upio was determined to call the old women to chant over her so she could be repossessed by the evil spirit and rebuild his little hut. But Uriemo got up from her bed and ran to Moro Sheeba's hut. There the two women knelt before the true God and asked for deliverance for the glory of His name. The next morning the heathen people were amazed to see Uriemo go back to her hut with the swelling completely gone.

There were two women at Awasi by the name of Mvoga. One of them was the wife of Moro's half brother, Rasham. This Mvoga resented every effort of her sister-in-law to teach her the words of God. She hated her so bitterly that she would "sing Moro" when she ground grain—one of the Alur ways of bringing a curse upon someone.

"My sister-in-law, Moro, is a very bad person. Let her die today," she would sing. *"Eh-yeh-yeh! Eh-yeh-yeh!"*

Again and again she would repeat her chant, interspersed with a few grunts as she rubbed her grinding stone rhythmically over the kernels of millet. The heathen women waited to see what Sheeba would do to retaliate. To their astonishment, it did not even make her angry. Instead she went to Mvoga after a little while with the request,

"Is the food cooked that was made with the flour over which my name was sung? Please give me some and let me eat it."

A heathen woman would not have dared to eat the mush made with that flour for fear of the curse. But Moro used this as a means to show Mvoga that she loved her. Finally Mvoga broke down before the testimony of her sister-in-law and turned to follow the same God that she worshiped.

The other Mvoga was a village sister of Moro's who had been purchased by Pilipili's brother Malali. She had been an ardent servant of Jok, possessed by an evil spirit, but she had become a Christian through the influence of Sheeba and Solimon Uminji. Malali too had turned to the true God. But he was distressed because his wife did not seem to be completely free from her old life.

"I am going to go and tell Sheeba that you are doing the works of Jok again," he warned her, and he did tell Sheeba.

"Who told you you should go back into captivity again?" Sheeba asked Mvoga after she had called her for a talk. "Leave the affairs of Jok and follow Jesus. Tomorrow we are going to Rubanga's village to burn the witchcraft of others who have believed in Jesus. I want you to go too."

Mvoga went with Sheeba to see the articles of witchcraft burned, but she did not take her own. That night she could not sleep because of the fetishes she had hidden in her hut. She was so miserable that the next day she took them to the long grass and threw them away. Then she knelt down and addressed Jok,

"Today I am leaving you, Jok. You are a liar and today I leave you."

From that day Mvoga ceased to serve Jok. The following day the men of the village burned off all the tall grass so that they could chase out the wild animals and kill them. They did not know it, but they burned Mvoga's Jok, and she was glad.

These and other women at Awasi came to believe in Moro Sheeba's God, and many of the men as well, because of the teaching of this humble woman who walked in their midst. Moro herself knew that this was the work of God and she gave Him all the glory, praising Him for allowing even a despised woman to be an instrument in His hands.

Chapter 14

"WHAT A FAITH SHE HAS!"

IT WAS EARLY on a Sunday morning in June over three years after Pilipili's return from the doctor on his own two feet. He had put on his old clothes and was leaving to join his three companions—Afuru, Pacumbe, and Rubanga. They were going to check on their *ugwa,* fish traps, which they had anchored out in the middle of Lake Albert—"the Big Lake," as Pilipili and his brother called it.

"Pilipili, don't go to check your *ugwa* on God's day! You are a Christian and you should go to the house of God on His day," remonstrated Moro Sheeba.

Simon Ugwoko, the evangelist-teacher, was on hand and backed up Moro's advice with a further word of exhortation.

"Sheeba is right," he said. "You should check your fish traps on a day of work."

"Shall I go alone?" asked Pilipili defensively. "The other three with whom I have joined insist on going on their free day. Do they not have to work the other days?"

In spite of Moro's protests and Simon's warning, Pilipili joined his three village brothers and soon they were tramping single file down the steep narrow path that led to their canoes, which they had left on the shore of the Big Lake. From force of habit, they took a cautious look around the water's edge to make sure no crocodiles were lurking there. Then they dragged their two little dugout canoes into the water. They must take two canoes in order to carry their catch, for these small canoes could carry only three people at the most.

Afuru and Pilipili climbed into one of the little canoes and Rubanga and Pacumbe into the other. They paddled out with great hopes, skillfully handling the crude paddles that propelled them farther and farther out into the lake, until they could see bobbing up and down in the water the sticks that showed them where they had let down their *ugwa*. But before they could reach the bobbing sticks, a strong wind came up, so strong that it made it difficult for them to keep the canoes right side up. Soon it was blowing violently. There was no time now to think of pulling in their catch. All hands were needed and every muscle must be strained to keep the little craft afloat. Suddenly a big wave struck the canoe in which Pilipili and Afuru were struggling, capsizing it and throwing them into the water.

Pilipili, who was a good swimmer, made for the overturned canoe and got a hold on it. He saw Afuru go under the water, come up, and go under again. Frantically Rubanga and Pacumbe paddled toward their comrades. Pilipili realized that the little canoe could take only one of them. Then, as he saw Afuru come to the top the second time, he made a quick decision.

"Afuru has gone under twice," he called to his partners. "Save him and take him to land. Then come back and get me."

Seeing that Pilipili was still hanging on to the side of the capsized canoe, they rushed toward Afuru and with great difficulty succeeded in getting him into their canoe. As quickly as their strength allowed, they paddled to the shore. When they had Afuru safely on land, they hurried back to the place where they had left Pilipili, but they could not see him. There was nothing to do but go back and get others to help look for him.

It was noon before they pulled their canoe ashore once more. Already Pilipili had been afloat for an hour. They must get help to him before his strength gave out and he let go of the canoe or a crocodile found him. They were exhausted themselves, but they saw someone on the shore.

"Go, go quickly to Pilipili's village," they commanded him. "Call his relatives to come and help search for him. His canoe turned over in the lake. The wind blew him away while we were saving Afuru. Go, go quickly!"

When the messenger burst into Upio p'Ajika's village with the news, his words brought consternation to everyone. Instantly the village was in an uproar. The air was rent with the agonized cries of the villagers.

"*Aka! Aka! Aka!* (Pilipili is dead!) *Wo-wo-wo-wo!*"

"*Aka-yo! Aka-yo!* (What shall we do!)"

"*Aka! Aka! Aka!*"

As Pilipili's brother Musasi, Simon the evangelist, Filipo, and others of Pilipili's village brothers rushed to the lake, the women, girls, and old people threw themselves about wildly and wailed. Who could be lost in the Big Lake and come out alive? But Moro Sheeba was not wailing. She sat quietly in her hut praying to the true God, with her Bible open in her hands.

"My Father, show Thy power to these people by restoring Pilipili to us that they may know that Thou art the true God," she prayed. "I know Thou art with me in this perilous time, and I trust Thee."

The news traveled fast and far. In no time at all the village of Awasi was teeming with outsiders. To this day Musasi recalls with disgust how the guests who came to wail for Pilipili ate up all his ants, a delicacy which he had laid up for himself in abundance during the season just past. The people were indignant at the attitude of a wife who could sit quietly in her hut on such an occasion, with a Bible in her hands.

"Eh, what kind of a woman are you," they asked, "that you do not wail when your husband is drowned in the lake?"

"Why don't you wail?"

"Why don't you break your cooking pots?"

Even Sheeba's own heathen relatives heard the news that day and hastened to her village to comfort her. But when they saw her, they screamed in exasperation,

"The Book of God! The Book of God! The Book of God! What is it that you should sit with the Book of God in your hands all the time and not even wail for your husband who has drowned?"

By all this Moro Sheeba was unmoved. An inward peace was reflected on her face as she told them again and again of her faith in the true God.

"I won't break my cooking pots. If God wants to take Pilipili, He will take him. If He wants him to return, he will return."

Nor was Moro Sheeba the only one who was being chided that day. Afuru, Pacumbe, and Rubanga, weary from the day's ordeal, had returned to the village only to be accused by the old men of having killed Pilipili. Afuru cursed the lake and vowed that he never would go near it again—and he kept that vow, though he lived more than fifteen years longer.

While this was going on in the village of Awasi, Musasi, Simon, and a great number of other men and women had reached the Big Lake. It was too late for them to go out on the water, so they sat on the shore hoping to catch the sound of Pilipili's voice crying for help, so that they would know where to go to rescue him. Some of the men slept at the lake, prepared to take off at daybreak, and Musasi had a big canoe in readiness, together with the four men who were needed to handle it. Many returned to the village, after listening in vain for the cry for help, while others were sent farther up the lake to see if Pilipili's body had been washed ashore.

Moro was praying at home, and all night long she was

scolded and scoffed at for refusing to wail for her dead husband. When daylight came, the people said to her,

"One who spends a night in the lake, can he be saved?"

"I do not sorrow as a heathen," was Moro's answer. "I believe in the Lord Jesus. I will wait and pray."

"If your God returns Pilipili to this village alive we will all believe," the people answered.

At the first streak of dawn, the men at the lake pushed and pulled the big dugout canoe into the water. They crawled into it and were off. Where? Only God knew. Was not Sheeba at home praying? They pushed out into the middle of the lake. All morning they paddled around looking, looking, always looking—but in vain. Noon came and there was no sign of Pilipili. Discouraged and almost ready to give up, Musasi took one more look. Away off on the horizon he saw a speck.

"Look, look," he cried to his fellow canoemen, "it looks as though that may be a person!"

With all their might the four men paddled the big canoe toward the speck. If they found Pilipili, could he possibly be alive?

"It is he! It is he!" they told one another excitedly as the speck began to take shape.

As they drew near, they could see that Pilipili was sitting in the little canoe laboriously dipping out water with his hands. He was a pitiful sight. His body was white from having spent much time in the water. His chest was covered with abrasions, from hours of constant rubbing on the rough exterior of the overturned canoe. He was scarcely recognizable, but he was alive. The true God had answered prayer!

Pilipili had clung to the capsized canoe all the afternoon of the day before and far into the night. Only God knew when his tireless efforts to right it had been rewarded. He had managed to get into it, but it was so full of water that at any minute it might have sunk. In spite of his bleeding chest and aching muscles, he had set to work dipping the water out of the canoe with his cupped hands. It was a slow process, but he was able to do it. Nor did he dare to stop dipping water, for the waves constantly splashed into the tiny canoe. It was amazing that his strength had held out until his rescuers sighted him, but he had prayed in the night as he lay across the capsized canoe. Now God was giving him another chance to live a faithful testimony to Him. It was true that he had grown cold and careless spiritually, but God was long-suffering with His wayward child.

The big canoe slid alongside the tiny one. Musasi and his village brothers lifted the exhausted Pilipili into the dry canoe. They emptied the little dugout of its water and one of them paddled it back to the shore, while the other three took Pilipili in. The word of his rescue created a greater sensation than that of his disappearance.

"Pilipili is found," the cry went up along the winding paths. "He is alive!"

"So that woman had reason for being brave! Her God is a strong God."

Quickly the news spread, like a grass fire. From everywhere men and women and boys and girls came running to the village of the subchief Upio p'Ajika.

"Is it true? Is it true?" they would ask. "Is Pilipili still alive?"

With mingled fear and awe, they saw him with their own eyes. Many of them began to praise the true God, for no one but a mighty God could perform such a miracle as to bring a man back to his village alive after a day and a night in the Big Lake. From that time on, many were afraid not to go to the house of God on God's day.

In a village, about halfway between Awasi and Ara, was a girl who had just eloped with a young man, whom she preferred to the one who had finished paying wealth on her to her parents. On the afternoon that Pilipili was lost in the Big Lake, she listened to the villagers of her new village exchanging news with people on the path.

"What's news?" they would ask in the customary way.

"There is no news," the travelers would answer. "Oh, there is a woman over at Awasi that has truly believed God. What a faith she has! Her husband is lost in the lake, but she hasn't broken her cooking pots. She hasn't wailed. She sits around reading her Book of God, and she prays, prays, prays. Surely she is a woman of great faith!"

Other travelers would give a different version, "*Eh,* what kind of woman is that, my relatives, who doesn't even wail when her husband is drowned in the lake! What kind of a faith is that? She thinks he will come to life out of the lake. What a fool she is!"

But the next afternoon when people passed on the path she heard them say, "You know that man who was drowned in the lake? Whose wife did not wail? She only read her Book and prayed? He has come back to life. What a faith! What a faith!"

So it came about that this young girl, with a multitude of others, first came in contact with a real faith in the true God. Little did she realize then that the woman of faith about whom she had just heard would lead her to accept the Lord Jesus as her Saviour and that some day she would be known as Salome, a woman of like faith.

But did all the people believe as they said they would if Pilipili came back alive? There were some who did, but there were many others who did not. They were like those of whom Abraham in the parable spoke to the rich man in Hades: "If they hear not Moses and the prophets, neither will they be persuaded, though one rise from the dead."

Chapter 15

THE BEGINNING OF *MONKWENDA*

AT THE BEGINNING of 1934, just a few months after the miraculous rescue of Pilipili from the waters of the Big Lake, the "white elders" of the missionaries set aside a missionary *madamo* to spend all her time in helping the African mothers. There were girls who had gone to school at the mission who were out in the villages in homes of their own. She would encourage them in doing the work of God. There were women in the villages who had believed. She would seek a way for them to be taught in the Book of God. There were countless wives and mothers still bound by the fearful chains of Jok, needing to hear the truth that would make them free. Moro Sheeba rejoiced in anticipation of what God was going to do for her downtrodden fellow women.

"What's news of the women?" she would ask of anyone who happened to pass through Awasi from Kasengu, where this missionary *madamo* lived.

The news that she heard was good. A Bible class had been organized just for the women. They met very early every Friday morning, early enough to get back to their gardens for a good day's work so they would not incur the displeasure of their husbands. Every Thursday the Christian women at Kasengu were walking in the nearby villages to invite other women to their class. The women were responding. Many of them were turning away from Jok to believe in the true God.

All that she heard made Moro long for the same thing to be done in her own village. Then one day a messenger from the missionary arrived at her door. The *madamo* wanted to know if there were women and girl believers at Awasi who would like to join in a canvas of the huts in the districts of Kasengu and Ara. Moro Sheeba was delighted, for this was the sort of thing which she loved most to do. With her characteristic enthusiasm for anything that would further the knowledge of the true God, she joined not one but several of the groups and went with them to different districts.

The groups were organized under the leadership of the men volunteers, each of whom was given a notebook in which to keep his records. A system of symbols was used, for some of these men did not know how to write. With a *rumia*[1] he would draw a circle to represent each hut. Certain marks within the circle indicated a man, a woman, and the number of children there. Other marks showed whether they were Christians or heathen, if they ever had heard the Gospel before, if they were interested, or if they were antagonistic.

Sheeba prayed with the missionary that God would do a work not only among those to whom they were going, but also for those who took part in the visitation, for many of the women were new in the faith. That prayer had a particular answer in the case of one old woman who had come to Jesus in the Kasengu Bible class. When this old lady went to join her group, she picked up her long-stemmed pipe and hid it in the folds of the unbleached muslin skirt which was her only piece of attire. No one had told her that she should give up her pipe, but as she followed her fellow women walking single file in the narrow path, she felt very uncomfortable because she had it with her. Her comrades, who were singing or chatting while they

[1]A local coin about the size of a U.S.A. quarter.

walked, little realized the terrific struggle that was going on in the poor old woman's heart. But at last her decision was made.

"I want to tell the people about Jesus and beg them to accept Him," she told herself, "but they will point to my pipe and will not believe. No, I cannot go with this pipe. But how can I get along without my smokes? For Jesus' sake I shall try for just the few days we are on this trip."

Having gained this measure of victory, she stooped over and hid her pipe in the tall grass, but in a safe place, carefully making note of where she had put it, for she intended to retrieve it on the journey home. However, the blessing which she received in winning a soul to her Jesus so far surpassed the pleasure she once had with her pipe that she related the incident upon her return with this joyful testimony,

"When I came back to the place where I had left my pipe, I went right past it without any desire to pick it up again. God took away my desire for that pipe. I am not going to smoke any more."

The information obtained through the hut-to-hut visitation revealed a great and urgent need among the spiritually neglected mothers in all the villages. So heavy was the burden of this need upon the heart of Moro Sheeba that she wanted to travel with the missionary *madamo* to every outpost in the Kasengu-Ara districts where evangelists were located, and help in the forming of Bible classes for women in each of them.

"Is not God's work very important?" was Pilipili's sympathetic response when she approached him on the subject. "I give you permission to walk in the villages, far and near, with the missionary. I will look after the children while you are gone. I cannot teach, but I can help in this way."

Women in the village, whom Moro had brought to Jesus, were also glad to lend a hand in cooking for her family while she was away, so she and the missionary began their work together, spending three weeks at a time in the villages, going from outschool to outschool. Many women would come to hear them out of curiosity to see the white woman, but their attention and interest were really clinched when they heard the testimony of an Alur woman who lived under the same curses as they did.

"This woman is like us," they would say. "She has a husband and three children at Awasi. She has gardens to care for. She knows all about the spirits of the dead and about Jok."

Thus they listened with open hearts to the story of how she had been freed from the bondage of Jok and had come to know and love the true God and Saviour of the world. They looked at her with wonder when she told them how she had been misunderstood and persecuted, but how the true God had stood by her and strengthened her, how God had made her husband a believer, so that now he was willing to stay home and care for the children because the words which she was telling them were so important for them to hear.

Hundreds of heathen women allowed their names to be written down as members of the Bible classes in the various districts. If there was one woman in the village who loved the Lord Jesus and could read, she was placed in charge of the class. If not, the evangelists would help until some woman could take over the responsibility. Sheeba and the missionary had to visit many of the heathen husbands in order to get permission for the women to attend these classes. Most of the men agreed, but some of the husbands were bitterly opposed to the whole affair, and their wives knew that they would get a beating every time they would attend.

"These are good-tasting words," these women would often say. "If Sheeba suffered for the sake of the true God, I too can suffer."

The classes began with seventeen foundation lessons that were handed to each teacher. At the mission station and on every outpost the women were studying the same lesson, memorizing the same verses from the Book of God, and learning the same hymn. They were urged to be faithful in attendance and diligent in learning, for there was to be a big gathering of all the women at Kasengu where their lessons would be reviewed and they would show what they had learned. When she was not traveling with the missionary, Moro Sheeba would visit the various classes to help the leaders and encourage the members, particularly if she heard of a class where things were not going too well.

A conference just for women was an unheard-of thing. Many wondered how women could leave their gardens and the work of their homes for three whole days. However, when the time came, several hundred women gathered at Kasengu and there was a representative from every Bible class. The women had ground flour and contributed beans to be used as sauce with their mush, sending or carrying in the food ahead of time. Moro Sheeba was active in the preparations at Kasengu along with the local women. The day before the conference began they waited on the paths leading to the mission station to welcome their guests and assist them with their loads.

At the very first session of this conference an organization came into being which was to have a widespread ministry among the women of Alurland. It was the *Monkwenda pa Yesu Kristu,* or "Women Messengers of Jesus Christ." Its purpose was to bind the Christian women together for mutual strengthening in Bible study, and mutual standing against the many temptations of life in a heathen village; and to seek avenues of service for Jesus Christ, especially in a united effort to reach the heathen women of their communities through systematic village visitation.

In order to carry out the work to which the women were giving themselves, some leaders would be needed. They would need to have an overseer for each of the eight outdistricts, and they would need to have a president. The duties of the overseers would be to visit the Bible classes in their districts—to teach, encourage, and help in any way they could, and to meet periodically with their president for report and prayer. The duties of the president would be to head up the work as a whole and to counsel with the overseers. The choosing of officers was an entirely new experience for the women, but there was no hesitancy on the part of any of them as to who the president should be. Moro Sheeba was their unanimous choice, and she, in her quiet, unassuming manner, happily accepted the office as a larger channel through which she might serve her Lord.

Chapter 16

MONKWENDA'S PRESIDENT

THERE WERE FEW WOMEN in Alurland in the early days of the *Monkwenda pa Yesu Kristu,* who had risen above their subservient background or grasped spiritual realities sufficiently to occupy the places of leadership in the new organization. Hence it was not easy to find an overseer for each of the eight districts. Moro Sheeba, however, was quick to recognize the latent possibilities in her fellow women. For the districts which seemed to have no one in readiness she encouraged some whom she knew could fill the place, until every district but one had an overseer. Unwilling to see that district neglected, Moro offered herself.

"Very well," she said, "if no one accepts the work of overseer in that district, I shall visit it until God raises up a leader from there."

In spite of the fact that the farthest outschool in that district was six hours' walk from Moro Sheeba's village, she gave herself untiringly to special help for that district until God answered prayer and raised up a woman who was able to take over the office of overseer. This was in addition to the responsibility which she carried as the president over all of the district overseers.

Always Moro had the staunch support of her friend Hana

Usiga, the little Pacuwegi who had carried her books when she first walked in the villages at Ara. Hana's husband, Solimon Uminji, was now the pastor of the Kasengu-Ara church. Their home at Kasengu was a spiritual haven for Moro Sheeba. It was there that she always stayed when she visited Kasengu. They too were burdened for the women, and many were the hours that they spent together in prayer for them. As long as Moro Sheeba lived, she and Hana were faithful friends who loved to give out the Word of God together.

When the work of *Monkwenda* started, Sheeba was led to call upon a bashful, retiring young woman by the name of Rebeka Nyalwiny to help as an overseer. At first she shrank from the very suggestion. As a young girl in the girls' boarding school on the mission station, Rebeka had been blessed by the messages from God's Word which Moro had given when she visited the school, and now she responded when Moro encouraged her to be bold in serving God and giving out His Word. Rebeka became a faithful assistant to Hana Usiga in the *Monkwenda* work at Kasengu, and through the years did much to further that work in the whole district.

Another of the overseers was a young woman who had been reared in the home of Hana Usiga, trained at the girls' school, and was living in one of the villages with her evangelist husband.

"Oh, Moro, I am very meek," she exclaimed when she was asked to take over the district in which she lived. "I could never do that work."

"Think of Solomon," the president reminded her. "When he told the Lord that he did not have wisdom to rule over the children of Israel, God heard his prayer and gave him great wisdom. He will do the same for you if you ask Him."

So this young woman also, taught and encouraged by Moro Sheeba, fellowshiped with her in the work for many years.

Anna *ci* Sungoma helped in the visitation in different districts and was overseer in the district near where Moro Sheeba lived. As a little girl of perhaps eight years, she had heard of the true God and believed in Him through the testimony of Yohana Ukumu, even before Moro had started to walk in the villages around Ara. When her parents died, she was sent away to her mother's relatives, one of whom took her to a faraway town and finally sold her to a white man from Zanzibar to be his wife. Before her first baby was born, while her husband was away, she ran off and went back to her home village. There she learned that an Alur man had purchased her, having started his payments while her mother and father were living. The big chief ruled that the white man could not have her and compelled her to go to her African husband whose name was Sungoma.

It was after Anna was married to Sungoma that she was brought back into the path of the true God and was baptized. In the persecutions which followed, Moro Sheeba was a pillar of strength to her, leading her on in her spiritual life. Anna became one of the stalwarts among the leaders of *Monkwenda,* along with Moro Sheeba and Hana Usiga.

One of the first things which Moro Sheeba had done when she returned to Awasi after the organization of *Monkwenda* was to appoint the evangelist-teacher's wife and Uriemo, the subchief's wife, to go into another district as hut-to-hut visitors. There they met with many a rebuff.

"*Eh-h-h!*" the people would say. "These women hand out the Gospel from door to door. Whoever heard of such a thing! You are bad people."

But the women kept on teaching, going regularly each Tuesday, inviting the women to attend prayer meeting on Wednesday and the weekly Bible class on Friday. As soon as a woman was *born again,* Moro Sheeba would take her along in visitation work to encourage her in soul-winning.

The *Monkwenda* groups met together occasionally in order

to receive further instruction in the Book of God, to pray, and to praise God for what He was doing for them. At one such gathering on Ara, Sheeba asked Uriemo, who was now baptized as Elizabeti, to go with her. At the same time her husband, Upio p'Ajika, was planning to attend a big dance and insisted that she go with him and dance. As a Christian, she could not enter into the sensual heathen dance, so she chose to go with Sheeba.

As she was sitting in the women's conference absorbed in the message from God's Book, Elizabeti Uriemo felt a tap on her shoulder and was told that someone outside desired to speak to her. She found Sheeba at her side as she faced a soldier sent by her angry husband.

"Your husband says you are to come home immediately and dance," the soldier informed her. "He says Sheeba is making you crazy."

The soldier said that Upio had cursed her with a much-feared curse and sent this message:

"Don't you dare come back to my hut if you refuse to go to the dance and dance. Go immediately to your home village and stay there. You may not enter my hut again."

Uriemo sent her husband as kind a message as she could, explaining that she did not want to be disobedient, but that she could not do the things that he asked her to do if they were against God's will, and that she could not dance.

"Come on, go back to your own hut. Do not be afraid," Moro Sheeba urged her when the meetings were over, so she and Moro went back to Awasi together. As she left Sheeba at her door and started down the path to her own hut, Sheeba called after her,

"Be sure that you have some good food cooked for your husband before he comes back."

Elizabeti Uriemo profited by this advice. Immediately she set abcut to prepare a delicious meal and had it all ready against her husband's return. Then she hurried over to Sheeba's hut and the two gave themselves to prayer. When Upio p'Ajika came home, he ate the food and did not bother his wife any more.

While Moro Sheeba was eager to go about among the women to impart to them a knowledge of the true God, she never lost an opportunity to learn more about Him herself—anywhere that the Word was being taught. When instruction classes and conferences were held for the teacher-evangelists she did not let the fact that she would be the only woman present deter her from attending and better equipping herself for the service of the Lord. Had she been a heathen woman going into a group of heathen men, she would have been thought very bold. But most of these Christian men praised her for they understood her motive, although a few who were not strong in the Lord themselves would ask,

"What is this woman bothering herself about, coming into our midst? Will she learn anything?"

But Moro conducted herself in a becoming way; she made careful notes of the helps which she received, for she wrote a beautiful hand and was very correct in spelling; and unconsciously she shed forth the fragrance of the Lord whenever she attended these classes. Many of the men leaders gave public testimony at different times to the blessing she had been to them, by her example in their midst.

When Moro Sheeba heard that three men in Mukambo were meeting once a week to study the Word of God, she took herself off to this class also, saying to the men,

"This is a good affair which you have started. Don't ever leave it. It will help others to understand the Word of God."

In this class, they would read the Book of God verse by verse, and then they would discuss it. Moro tried to get other women to join her, but at first she was successful in getting only Anna *ci* Sungoma to come. However, God's hand of blessing was upon that class, and Moro Sheeba had much to do with its growth. In time it became a large class with men, women, boys, and girls in attendance. They would go through the entire New Testament verse by verse, taking years to complete it, and then they would start at the beginning and go through again. Christians in other parts of the country heard of the blessing received, and similar classes were started elsewhere. In each instance Sheeba encouraged the women to attend so that they too would grow in the Lord.

In the conferences which the *Monkwenda* held in different parts of the country, Moro Sheeba was always there to share in the blessings and also to impart a blessing to others. To one of these conferences came a young woman whose husband had been assigned as an evangelist to that district. This woman had heard of Moro Sheeba but had not met her before. She noticed that all the other women were busy talking, but that Moro Sheeba was quiet and that part of the time she sat with her head bowed. Later she learned that she was praying for God's blessing on that gathering.

When the evangelist of that particular village came to greet the women guests, he wanted to do something fine to welcome them.

"I must find a goat," said he to Moro Sheeba, "and kill it for you and for the *Monkwenda.*"

"Oh! Oh! Isn't it great," the women said, elated that they were to have this treat in place of the bean sauce that they usually ate with their staple mush. "We are going to eat meat. We are going to eat meat."

Moro looked up searchingly at the teacher-evangelist.

"No," she told him. "You are not going to kill a goat for us. We have not come to eat meat. We will find our reward in Heaven."

The women were amazed at her answer. But they realized that their leader was one who was so interested in spiritual things that the things of this world were not too attractive to her. Gently she rebuked them,

"Women, you are laughing and joking about the meat. Laughing and fun are not wrong, but let us put our hearts on the meat that is of Heaven."

Yet Moro Sheeba was not one to neglect the practical needs of the women. Late at night, after the meetings were over and the rest of the women were tired and resting, some of them sleeping, she and Anna *ci* Sungoma would cook some food and then call them to eat.

So it was that the God-centered, self-sacrificing life of their president made a deep impression on all the women of *Monkwenda.* When they saw that no distance was too great for her to travel if she could help a soul, encourage a leader, or gain a deeper knowledge of the Book of God, they sought to follow her example that they might learn more of the Saviour who had made Sheeba's life so influential in each of their own.

Chapter 17

THE *AGULU* OF GOD

As THE CHRISTIAN WOMEN grew bolder in the united witness which they bore to their belief in the true God, they were equally ready to show their faith by good works. When the hut of one of the women believers at Awasi burned down, Sheeba suggested that the *Monkwenda* might like to help her. Great was the response. Women came to her with earthen pots, baskets small and large, brooms, gourds for water, and many other household articles. The heathen looked on and marveled at what the love of God caused His children to do, for such a thing never was heard of before the Gospel came to Alurland.

A general time of suffering at Awasi gave the *Monkwenda* another opportunity to demonstrate their love. The government official at Mahagi had sent his clerk to take a census of the people there, and at the same time Chief Abok had sent his clerk to collect the taxes. While the census was being taken, the clerks discovered a man whom the government had been wanting and immediately took him prisoner. In his fight with the soldier who tied him, the man managed to cut the soldier's head with a small hoe.

The affair grew to serious proportions when it was misrepresented to Chief Abok by his clerk and others, who told him that the people of Awasi had killed all his soldiers. Abok became very angry and sent soldiers there because he thought the people were defying his authority. They took corn, peanuts, grain, francs, blankets, axes, and hoes from the people. They killed their goats and chickens and ate them. Men grabbed one another on the path, tearing off each other's clothes and beating up one another.

Seeing that many were left without clothes, food, or implements for working their gardens when this affair was over, the *Monkwenda* rallied around, eager to show their love to the Lord Jesus by helping their fellow men. Their ministry at this time was a particularly strong testimony because they made no difference among those they helped, supplying the needs of believers and heathen alike, an action so contrary to native custom that many became interested in the message of the true God which these women propagated.

Not the least of the women's ministrations were to Moro Sheeba herself. So grateful were they for her spiritual help that they would come and help her with a big weeding job, or with other tasks, so that she might be free to walk among them —for Moro never was one to neglect her home duties.

Moro Sheeba had been a constant example of faithful tithing before all the church members down through the years.

"Before the church even talked about it, my mother tithed," Daniel says of her.

When she brought her grain in from the field, immediately she would measure out the Lord's part and take it to the little church. When she sent out her children to sell peanuts, she would count out a tenth of the money they brought back, and on the following Sunday morning she placed it in the "box of God." Now that she and the other *Monkwenda* were realizing the blessing that was brought by their ministrations to the needy, they embarked upon a further course of giving.

It was announced at the big annual *Monkwenda* conference

that each Christian woman was to have in her hut an *agulu,* an earthen vessel, for God. In this she would place gifts for God beyond her tithing. Every day when she ground her flour, she was to put a handful or two in God's *agulu.* Periodically the contents of all their *agulus* were to be gathered together and sold. The proceeds were to be used in helping others, for Jesus' sake.

In one district, the women gathered a large amount of grain and flour, but there was no place to sell it. Then they prayed and the Lord provided a market for it. They used the money it brought to help the poor in their communities, and some of it to buy beans for a big *Monkwenda* conference to which guests had been invited. In Kasengu district was a very old woman to whom they gave food from the *agulu* of God, which subsequently led her to believe in Him. There was an evangelist with a large family, who was so poor in health that he had difficulty in getting large enough gardens dug to provide the necessary food. The women used the food in their *agulus* to help him. Many, many old folk were helped in this way, and their hearts were touched as they listened to the message of God's love, even if His servants were only women—for it was an unheard-of thing to help anyone who was not a blood relative.

One time the women of Anna *ci* Sungoma's district had a good supply of flour and grasshoppers, but could find no place to sell them. They contributed the grasshoppers, a prized delicacy, to an evangelists' conference on Ara. Then word came of an old, old woman who lived away across the Kakoi River and who was very, very needy. The women added millet, salt, and locusts to their collection of flour, and Anna started out with two other *Monkwenda* women to help carry the loads.

When they arrived in the village where the old woman lived they went first to the evangelist's hut, but the people were all in the little mud chapel having a service. They inquired for the old woman, whose name was Nyamalu and who professed to be a believer, but she was not inside the church. She was sitting outside behind it in a place where she could hear the words that were being taught, afraid to go in because the children might make fun of her—for the poor old soul was only skin and bones and she had a bad cough.

Old Nyamalu led Anna and her friends down a narrow path through the elephant grass to her dilapidated hut. It had fallen down, but she had propped it up with poles. The women went in and swept it, one of them carried a pot of water from the stream, and then they sat down and began to teach her from the Book of God.

"Do not try to serve two masters," they told her. "You have believed in Jesus. Have you cast away all the witchcraft you used to have? If you believe in Jesus, throw it away so that Jok will not come back to trouble you again."

Nyamalu pointed up to the top of her hut to a gourd, telling the women to get it because her witchcraft was in that. She kept the fetishes of many other people as well as her own, and they were all in the gourd with hers. She told the women that they could throw her things away and that she no longer would keep those which belonged to others. After they had prayed with Nyamalu, they took the fetishes of the other people to the evangelist with instructions for him to return them to their owners.

"We have gone and taught Nyamalu often," said the evangelist to Anna and the other women, "and she said that she had believed Jesus, but we did not know that she had witchcraft. What did you teach her that made her bring it out?"

Once again it was the kindness shown by strangers, who fixed up her little hut and left her with good things to eat that made an old woman, steeped in the witchcraft of her tribe, cast away all faith in Jok and truly follow the living God. So the *Monkwenda* always were on the alert for needy people as they found that the ministry of material things opened their hearts for spiritual help. The *agulu* of God became a constant means of blessing as the women filled and emptied, and filled and emptied, the little earthen vessels again and again for Him.

Chapter 18

"A SUCCORER OF MANY"

THE DESIRE OF MORO'S YOUNG HEART at the time of her baptism had been that she might follow in the steps of the godly woman by whose name she had chosen to be called. Those who knew Moro Sheeba in her mature years could find no more fitting words with which to sum up the ministry of her life than those written of the first Phebe, that she was "a servant of the church" and "a succorer of many," for she never tired of doing for others.

Among the "many" whom she "succored" was an old blind man whose relatives had left him in a hut to die, without food or water. When Moro heard of it, she took food and wood for fire to this old man as long as he lived. Each time she visited she told him of the love of Jesus; and touched by her tender care the old man became a believer before he died.

When the hut of a witch doctor was struck by lightning, he was killed and his wife was severely burned. Before medicine could be procured for her, the woman's burns were in a very bad state. However, Moro walked a long distance each day to apply the medicine until the wounds were healed. This woman too learned to love the true God through the Word which Moro Sheeba taught her.

At some distance from Awasi was a woman believer who was struck by lightning, but who survived the experience. Those around her were very much afraid, and when her hair grew long and her head needed shaving, no one would do it for her lest some calamity befall them. When Sheeba learned of this poor woman's plight, she traveled miles to get to her, then fearlessly shaved the hair of her head, assuring the women that no harm would come to them. Weaker Christians, seeing what she had done, became stronger in their faith.

Old Nyarubaru was a pathetic soul, whom she longed to bring to a knowledge of her Saviour and for whom she labored long. When Nyarubaru's husband had died, she had returned to her home village Awasi with her three children. But her husband's people took all of her children away from her, and she was left alone. She was under a curse also for having given birth to twins. Remembering her own mother and the curses which had followed her all the days of her life for having borne twin boys, Moro Sheeba tenderly sought to show Nyarubaru how she could be delivered from this bondage.

In time Sheeba and Pilipili saw that Nyarubaru was quite needy, so they took the responsibility of supporting her. Sheeba would cook food and take it to her, and with each gift of food she would say to Nyarubaru,

"Believe in Jesus with all your liver."

It was a great joy to her finally to hear Nyarubaru's simple confession of faith,

"I believe in Him with all my liver. I leave all in His hands."

Immediately the old woman took off her *aminda,* the sign of having borne twins, which she wore to protect her from sickness and death. She handed over the *agulu kurugu* also, the double-mouthed earthen pot of the twins to which she had sacrificed at times of sickness. Sheeba watered this frail plant for her Master, and her faithfulness was rewarded, for old Nyarubaru made public confession of faith by baptism, taking the name of Maria. She became a real companion to Sheeba in the things of the Lord, and it was old Maria Nyarubaru who became the mainstay of Sheeba's home in later days when she herself was laid aside by sickness.

Typical of the many to whom Moro Sheeba administered spiritual succor was young Uringi. Uringi was a new babe in the faith when the man who had purchased her came to take her out of the girls' boarding school. She was still too bound by the customs in which she had been reared to seek the release that the government would have granted her from a man who already had other wives, so she offered no objections. But as she began her married life in the heathen village of Arobe, she could not give up the path of light in which she had begun to walk at Kasengu, and she inquired for a teacher of the words of God. When told that the nearest one was in Awasi, nearly an hour's walk away, she was "eaten" with such a desire to meet with the people of God that she went regularly in spite of the distance. It was there that she came into close touch with Moro Sheeba.

When Uringi's first child sickened soon after birth and died after she had refused to sacrifice for him, she was much berated by her family, who accused her of killing the child. But this was only the beginning of sore trials. Very soon she was looking forward to having another little one, and the time of his conception brought both mother and baby under a dreaded curse. The anxious relatives tried to do all they could to save the life of the unborn babe, who would be known as a "child of *ukumu.*" Her mother-in-law stood over her with a gourd of lizard's blood and beer, urging and demanding that she drink it—"to save our child's life."

"Oh," thought Uringi, "it is not as easy as I thought it would be. I've done wrong by marrying this heathen man, but I know there is a true God. He is Moro Sheeba's God, and He is my God. I will look to Him, and He will help me."

Her refusal to drink the heathen concoction marked the beginning of severe persecution from her husband and his people.

The witch doctor who had been called to perform the ceremony with the lizard's blood warned her not to shave the hair off her head, for that was the law of bearing a child of *ukumu.* If her hair was to be shaved, or that of the baby after it was born, she must visit the witch doctor with a goat. If anyone else did it for them, she and the baby would die.

Uringi's hair got long and shaggy. No one save a woman who was under a curse wore her hair like that. As soon as she could get to Awasi the unhappy girl went to Moro Sheeba and told all about her testings. After listening with sympathy, Moro suggested that Uringi go with her to the *Monkwenda* conference at Ara. She was hungry for Christian fellowship, so she went along. As she sat in the meetings, she heard the challenge for a completely surrendered life and saw such a life exemplified in many of the women about her. She thought of her shaggy hair, of the curse that kept it so, of the child of *ukumu* to whom she would give birth. Yet she yearned to respond to the challenge of fully following Jesus the Saviour. Fear was overcome at last as love for Him prevailed, and up went Uringi's hand in response to the invitation at the close of one of the meetings.

"*Afoyo Mungu* (I praise God)," said Moro Sheeba fervently when she saw the raised hand.

"*Aka yo!*" said Uringi to Moro and others after the service. "Even though my husband and his people kill me, I must have my head shaved."

She lost no time in attending to the matter. As she sat on the grass outside the little church, her legs outstretched, her head bent forward and her hands clasped over it, a group of women gathered around her. They too had heard the Gospel and believed. But in the hearts of some was fear as they heard Uringi declare her purpose to defy the heathen curse of *ukumu.* They looked askance at one another, and inconspicuously beat their chests with their hands as they nodded their heads rhythmically in the characteristic Alur gesture of amazement and fright.

There were others present who had dared to take such a stand themselves and who encouraged Uringi, reminding her that the life of her unborn babe was in the hands of the true God. Anna *ci* Sungoma doubled up her skirts between her legs, squatted on a little stool behind Uringi, and pulled the girl toward her. The onlookers followed every movement of her hand as she touched the shaggy hair with a razor blade. Uringi's heart was at peace and her countenance showed it. Had not Moro Sheeba gone through many testings more severe than this? Had God ever failed Moro? No, He had not—and Moro's God was her God too.

Uringi's return to her husband's village with her head shaved created a sensation which made her the subject of everyone's curses. The day after her return, Arobe went hunting and cut his foot on a stick. He came back and beat Uringi.

"Was it not because you shaved off your hair that I had this accident?" he growled at his young wife.

Again the persecuted young Christian ran to Awasi and poured out her heart to Moro. Moro read to her from the Book of God and encouraged her to remain true.

"And when you give birth to your child," she told her, "be strong in the faith. Don't let them take you out by a hole."

Uringi went back to bear a faithful testimony, and the Lord helped when it came time to give birth to Ukumu. When the days of her confinement were finished, she refused to let her people call the witch doctor to bring her out by a hole in the back of the hut, as giving birth to a child of *ukumu* required. Instead she prayed, and alone she brought her child out by the door of the hut. Her faith was strengthened as she saw God's hand of protection upon her, but when she washed the woolly head of little Ukumu, her heart would say,

"Can I not trust God to keep my baby too? God gave him to me, and He wants me to bring him up for Him."

She counted the cost, made her decision, and paid the price in the storm of persecution that broke upon her at home. But what rejoicing there was among those who no longer feared the curses that once bound them, when Uringi came to a gathering of the people of God at Kasengu and requested that little Ukumu's head be shaved!

While Moro Sheeba was sharing the burdens of others through their testings and rejoicing in their victories, she was by no means free from similar battles in her own family even though many of the people at Awasi had come to believe in her God. There was contention because a number of years had passed after the birth of Rodia and yet she had borne no more children although she was still a comparatively young woman. The men of Awasi were sure that she had displeased the spirit of her dead father Gem, and that he might be keeping her from having children. They wanted to take a goat to her home village to sacrifice to his spirit. Even her own village relatives became concerned. A village brother of hers came to visit her saying,

"See here, my sister, you have stopped bearing while you are still young because, when the wealth was paid on you, your husband's people did not give a goat to be sacrificed to the spirit of your ancestors. Even though you are a Christian, you can give a goat. We will sacrifice it and eat it. I will not sprinkle the water on you. We will just scold the spirit in your presence and then leave you."

But Sheeba would not listen to such a thing.

"If God wants me to have only these children, there is no affair," she kept telling him. "If He wants me to have more, He will give them."

Pilipili stood firmly with his wife and refused to give a goat for sacrifice. The matter was taken to the true God in prayer and left with Him. After a time the gossipers in the villages were busy, and their "insides burned much" with astonishment.

"What!" they exclaimed one to another. "Has Sheeba become an expectant mother without having sacrificed!"

Early one July morning in 1937, during a cloudburst, a messenger arrived at Kasengu to call on the missionary for help. Sheeba had given birth to another daughter, but all was not well. Hana Usiga and the missionary set out for Awasi as fast as possible, but there was a steep escarpment to descend and a stiff climb on the other side of the valley, so it was nearly two hours before they reached Moro's side. They found her sitting in her hut comforting the women who had gathered around her. Some of them had become excited and wanted to wail, but she had exhibited such an unmovable faith in God that they were sitting, quietly waiting to see how God would undertake for her.

Moro had taken care of the baby herself, wrapped her in a cloth, and laid her on a mat—a thing which no heathen woman would have dared to do—so the missionary and Hana gave all their attention to Moro. The Lord blessed their efforts, and it was not long before everything was all right. Then they turned to admire the new little girl.

"It is God's will that I have this child," said her mother tenderly. "She shall be called *Kayenyparwott,* Will-of-the-Lord."

Chapter 19

FROM CONGO TO GLORY

IT WAS NOT LONG after the birth of little Will-of-the-Lord, Kayeny, as she was called for short, that Moro Sheeba's body became greatly weakened by tuberculosis. The heathen at Awasi said that her sickness was being caused by the man and woman who, long before, had left the evil omens at her door. But she continued to befriend these two old folk in spite of the protests of her people.

Sheeba's passion for souls never abated. As long as she had the strength to do so, she went out every afternoon to teach in the villages. When she could no longer walk, she taught everyone who came to see her. She realized that she did not have much strength left, so she determined to make one more trip to encourage the women believers and to say good-by to the people of her brother Mugasa's village. Thin and weak as she was, she made the journey on foot, although it took her many hours.

On the way to her home village, Moro stopped at the village where Anna *ci* Sungoma taught the women's Bible class. Many had gathered to hear her speak. They all sensed that this might be the last time they would be meeting with her, and she made a lasting impression on them as she pleaded once more with the unbelievers to come to Jesus and urged the believers to continue steadfast in the faith.

"We do not understand death, do we?" she remarked to Anna

after the meeting. "I thought that Pilipili was to go first because of the great sickness which he has. But my strength is little now. I think I shall go first."

When she got to her home village, she gathered the women together and told them about the testing she had had by the man and woman in Pilipili's village who had left the evil omens at her door. Perhaps she did this because of the recent accusations made by his people and a fear lest her people attempt a belated retaliation. Then she took the Word of God and said to them,

"Listen, listen to the Word that made me forgive this evil act."

She showed them from the Book of God how they too could stand against such testings if they believed in Jesus. Earnestly she pleaded with them all to come to Him, to suffer persecution for Him if necessary—and they listened with awe because they knew that she was not telling them to do something that she had not already done herself.

After this trip Moro Sheeba's strength gave out rapidly. All the women loved her, and when she was no longer able to be up, many came and sat by her bedside crying because it grieved them to see her suffer.

"Don't cry for me," she would tell them. "When I go to be with the Lord, I want to go quietly."

There was one who did not wail but whose devotion was expressed in ceaseless ministrations to her as she lay on her sickbed. It was old Maria Nyarubaru, whom Sheeba had succored for so many years and whom she had expected to look after to the end of her days. Now the situation was reversed. It was Maria who cooked the food for Sheeba's family, who cared for little Kayeny, who tended the sick one as she became more and more feeble. The relatives did not now attempt to force her to sacrifice.

"Perhaps the missionary doctor at Rethy could help Sheeba," they said instead.

So the relatives of Sheeba and Pilipili worked together to make a hammock in which to carry her to the doctor. It was early in the spring of 1939 that they set out with her on the rugged journey that she had taken twice with her sick. After many miles of walking the men began to grow weak from hunger. Mugasa had them put Sheeba down on the ground and rest while he went to a nearby village where he bought two big bunches of bananas. He divided the bananas among the others but his own heart was so sad that he could not eat. This did not go unnoticed by his sister.

"What! Why are you not eating?" she asked him. "If you do not eat, you will not have strength to carry me. See, I have left my home—that home"—she pointed back to Awasi—"but I am going to my real home in Heaven."

After she had said that, Mugasa ate a little and she seemed satisfied. It was late in the afternoon when they arrived at Rethy. Sheeba was placed immediately in the hospital. Daniel, who was now a lad of fifteen, and her brother Baru's two daughters, whom she had helped to bring up after their father died, stayed to help care for her. Faithful old Maria looked after little Will-of-the-Lord.

Moro Sheeba's time at Rethy was short, but she witnessed constantly while she was there. Everyone who went to see her during her last days saw how she clung to her Bible. Always it would be in her hands or right by her side. If she were lying down, it would be under her head. Mugasa's little ten-year-old grandson Sila was in the hospital seriously ill at the same time. As he neared death, she could hear him in another room crying out at the top of his voice, and no one was able to quiet him. Sheeba pulled herself out of bed and made her way to the boy. She sat down beside him with the Book of God in her hand and spoke to him,

"Child of my brother, I thought perhaps I would get to Heaven before you, but you may arrive before I do. The important thing is to be sure that there is a place ready for you there. You must believe in Jesus. When you get there, look for my place too, for I am coming."

The child soon had peace and the joy of the Lord in his own heart. An Uncle was the only other relative who lived near enough to get to Sila before he died. The little boy held out his hand and bid him good-by.

"That is right," Moro told him. "You do well to say good-by, for you are going to a wonderful place. You are going to Heaven."

"I'm leaving you. I'm going to eat the feast of the Lamb," added the boy triumphantly.

While she was at the hospital, Moro sought to make one more gesture of kindness to an old woman in Mukambo whom she loved but whom everyone else had given up as hopeless and from whose hand they feared to eat. This woman was greatly moved when Sheeba had her son write her a note, asking that she send her something to eat. Quickly the woman ground flour and prepared chicken and mush for her, for Moro always enjoyed eating chicken even though the other Alur women feared to eat it lest they become barren.

When Hana Usiga and Solimon Uminji learned that Moro Sheeba was at Rethy, Solimon took the long journey over the mountains to comfort her and to have a last visit with her. He was shocked to see the emaciated condition of her body, but her face was radiant, and he was the one who received the comfort as she gave him Isaiah 41:10 to strengthen his hands in the Lord—a verse which became stamped indelibly on his mind and heart.

Elizabeti Uriemo and another of the Awasi women could not resist going to Rethy for one more glimpse of the one who had led them out from the bondage of Jok into the freedom in Jesus. When they arrived, Elizabeti started to take the hood off the baby which she had on her back. Always mindful of the comfort of others, Moro Sheeba stopped her.

"Do not take the hood off the baby," she remonstrated. "It is very cold here at Rethy. The baby might take cold."

As she talked to these women she encouraged them never to leave the Word of God, saying to them as they left her to return to Awasi,

"Women, do not get cold in the work of the Lord. Do not let the work of God die. Do not think about my death. If you really believe in Jesus, we shall be together some day."

Daniel was most devoted to his mother during her illness, and sensed the seriousness of the situation. Every day he would slip out into the tall grass to pray, for he knew that new responsibilities would fall upon him when she was gone. Sheeba realized that it would not be long before Pilipili would join her in her heavenly home, so it was to Daniel that she must entrust the spiritual care of her family. Matayo was a promising boy just entering his teens, whom she had nurtured carefully in the Lord. Sheeba's greatest concern when she was dying was for young Rodia, who was nine years old. Rodia always had been a difficult child to manage, stubborn and bent on having her own way, though it was a year since she had given her heart to Jesus after a hard struggle.

"Don't ever leave the path of God," she told Rodia at the last. "Look to Daniel even as you would look to me."

And to Daniel she said, "Now I am going to be with the Lord. I leave the care of my children in your hands. You must lead them straight in the path of God. If you fail, that will be your sin."

After she had spoken to her children and bidden them goodby, while the doctor, two African nurses, her husband, and others who loved her stood with the children around her bedside, Moro Sheeba spoke only a few more words, then closed her eyes and her spirit slipped away to be with Jesus. A life of less than forty years had been hers, yet such was the touch of the divine hand upon that life that no monument is needed to keep its memory alive. The years have not effaced the marks of its touch in the hearts and huts of the villages where she walked with the Book of God.

Chapter 20

HER WORKS DO FOLLOW HER

YEARS HAVE PASSED and changes have come to the Congo, but life in the backward places of Alurland goes on much as it did in Moro Sheeba's day, though some of the old faces are missing.

Pilipili, Matayo, and old Maria Nyarubaru have joined Moro in her heavenly home. Spiritually her mantle has seemed to fall upon Daniel, for God is blessing multitudes of young men through his ministry in the school for boys at Kasengu. He has carried out the charge that was given him by his mother and is seeking to lead his own little family in the knowledge of God, deeply grateful for the influence of her godly life upon his own. Little Kayeny, who was less than two when her mother left her, is growing up into a young woman whose quiet, unassuming ways are a sweet reminder of that mother.

In the village of Awasi stands a government rest house on the site of Moro Sheeba's old hut. Just a few yards away a big cloth tree, which she planted as a seedling on the grave of baby Yohana, gives shade to passers-by and the Christians who gather at the village chapel. On the porch of the rest house sits the missionary *madamo,* surrounded by people who knew and loved Moro. Upio p'Ajika is there, with his wife, Uriemo. Mugasa, old as he is, has come over from his home village. Anna *ci* Sungoma and many of the *Monkwenda* are present. They know that what they are telling the missionary is going to be written in a book to be read in the white man's land and each is eager to add some almost forgotten incident.

"We all of us believed in Jesus because of Sheeba. She led us to the Lord," is the testimony of the women who have gathered from far and near.

"It is as though Sheeba herself were in our midst again," they tell one another as they recall the events that are to be recorded in her life story, challenged afresh by the steadfastness of her faith in the face of the persecutions which they remember, by the fearlessness of her testimony, and by her tireless efforts to lead them out of darkness. For some who have grown careless in the ways of the Lord, it is the turning point back to blessing in Him.

Uringi is there. Her baby Ukumu has grown to young manhood, a living evidence of the power of the true God over the curses of Jok. Uringi has borne other children to Arobe, but since the affair of shaving Ukumu's head he has not persecuted her in the matter of sacrificing. He never has given up insisting that she make beer, however. With her head hung in shame, she confesses to the missionary *madamo* and some of the *Monkwenda,*

"Arobe demands that I make beer. I am ashamed to tell you, but I make it for him now. I even drink it myself sometimes. Ask God to give me strength to refuse everything that mars my witness for God who has been so faithful to me."

The *Monkwenda* understand. How many of them have not passed this rugged way, even as Moro Sheeba did? Have they not banded together to strengthen the hands of their fellow women in the same difficult position as Uringi? Were it not for their mutual prayers and encouragement, how many of them would stand utterly alone, unmoved by the taunts and threats of friends and relatives alike in the endless demands of the heathen society around them? Property of their men, bought with sheep and goats and cows to serve them, some of them able only haltingly to read the words of the Book of God that has brought true light to their once-darkened hearts and turned their love to Jesus—they make a tender appeal for the prayers of their fellow women in the faith the world around.

The Author

The third of five children, Beatrice Tannehill King was born of Christian parents on a farm in Kansas. During grade school days at the age of nine she definitely accepted Christ as her personal Saviour. Then followed high school and activity in church work as a Sunday school teacher and in the young people's society. When a sophomore the missionary call came to Beatrice through a sermon entitled, "To Every Man His Work." Her high school history teacher had deepened the missionary impact by speaking of the value of the work of missionaries to the government in Africa. There was a battle against surrendering to the call, but the young woman finally made her decision and had peace of mind. During years of preparation Ezekiel 3:18, 19 kept her goal in sight. The marriage of her sister and a car-train accident which invalided her mother brought household responsibilities and the need to become employed even during vacation recesses in order to complete her education and help relieve the financial burdens Beatrice's father was carrying in paying for medical care and doctors. It became imperative finally to break the news of her plan to go to Africa to her family, but God had prepared the way so that approval was given for the necessary Christian training. In 1923 study began at the Bible Institute of Los Angeles under the teaching of Dr. R. A. Torrey. With the exception of her last term, which was under a scholarship, it was necessary to work to pay expenses. After Los Angeles came graduation from medical missionary training at the National Bible Institute of New York, which training was also financed by her employment as a secretary. On September 7, 1926, Beatrice Tannehill sailed for the Belgian Congo where she is now serving. In May, 1930, Miss Tannehill became Mrs. Harvey J. King. In May, 1932, Mr. King was stricken with blackwater fever and was called to his heavenly Home.

Because of Mrs. King's work with the mothers and daughters of Africa, also her sharing with Moro Sheeba in beginning a work among the women, it is not difficult to understand her reason for desiring to share this excellent account of Moro Sheeba's life.